Siblings by Choice

Siblings by Choice

Race,
Gender,
and
Violence

Archie Smith Jr.
Ursula Riedel-Pfaefflin

CHALICE ®
PRESS
ST. LOUIS, MISSOURI

Biblical quotations, unless otherwise noted, are from the *New Revised Standard Version Bible*, copyright 1989, Division of Christian Education of the National Council of the Churches of Christ in the United States of America. Used by permission. All rights reserved.

Excerpts from *The Jerusalem Bible*, copyright 1966 by Darton, Longman & Todd, Ltd., and Doubleday, a division of Bantam Doubleday Dell Publishing Group, Inc. Used by permission.

Cover art: Getty Images
Cover and interior design: Elizabeth Wright

This book is printed on acid-free, recycled paper.

Visit Chalice Press on the World Wide Web at
www.chalicepress.com

10 9 8 7 6 5 4 3 2 1   04 05 06 07 08 09

Library of Congress Cataloging–in–Publication Data

Smith, Archie, 1939-
  Siblings by choice : race, gender, and violence / Archie Smith, Jr. & Ursula Riedel-Pfaefflin.
      p. cm.
  Includes bibliographical references and index.
  ISBN 0-827234-56-2 (pbk. : alk. paper)
  ISBN 978-0-827234-56-2
  1. Church work with minorities. 2. Marginality, Social—Religious aspects—Christianity. I. Riedel-Pfaefflin, Ursula. II. Title.
  BV4468.S65 2004
  261.8—dc22
                                                          2004011565

Printed in the United States of America

Dedicated to our parents & grandparents

Amos & Callie; Archie Sr. & Beatrice; Clara and Paula; and Erika

To siblings Marjorie, Leonard, Joyce and Geraldine

To children Tycho and Vincent

To the memory of Dennis Hunter Jr. and Rosalie June Potter

Contents

Preface

Rarely does a volume embody so clearly the invitation it sets forth to the world. *Siblings by Choice: Gender, Race, Violence* is the exception. In its pages the authors ask us to consider a life where we who have been enemies work together as brothers and sisters intent on mending the world. As the authors paint for us the portraits of their own social locations, we realize that they themselves represent the differences about which they speak—one an African American male who has known the systemic oppression of life in a White privileged society; the other a German female who has known privilege because of race, but oppression because she is woman. Being of different genders, races, and nationalities, they write together in the midst of a world broken and scarred by fear and violence.

It is not only from their own perspectives that they speak, however. Realizing that their own understandings are limited, they call on their many conversations with colleagues, women and men around the globe, in an effort to understand the myriad ways that gender and race, and other differences as well, create tensions and provoke violence among us. The volume is shockingly and brutally honest as it puts before us the raw realities of life. We would be overwhelmed if there were not a persistent, sometimes latent and sometimes explicit, hope that undergirds its writing. It is obviously not a naive hope that blinds itself to the grimness of war, fear, and the mistrust so prevalent across our borders. It is a God-given hope that is born in the imaginations of those who are willing to risk investment in a new way of being.

How, then, shall we live? That is the perennial question addressed here, but the volume shakes us from any answers that are limited to the personal, the individual, the internal. These are too narrow. Consistently, the volume demands that we look at the many ways that the personal is political and the political is personal, to consider the ways that the historical, social, political, economic, and ecological dimensions of the world form and fashion what we want to do, what we can do, what we hope to do in the world around us. It acknowledges that we are guided by what we see and the historical, invisible forces that we cannot. Thus, the volume is systemic to its core. We cannot help but realize through its reading that, whether we like it or realize it, the struggle must be ours—together. We are bound together in a "mutual garment of destiny."

Siblings by Choice returns again and again to three major themes or strategies that can be used as lenses for our study and consideration: systemic thinking, intercultural realities, and narrative agency. Over and again they are used by the authors as the lenses through which they analyze case studies and life situations that they, and we, encounter. Each return to them bears new insight, so that their repetition is not stagnant or purposeless. Rather, with each engagement a new layer of understanding is unleashed, and the interplay between the three grows organically and in geometric proportion. One begins to sense how much there is to observe, describe, and interpret in a world that is complex and ever changing.

Staggering are the many arenas for conversation that are brought to the fore in this volume. Smith and Pfaefflin call on the worlds of film, art, myth, history, the social sciences, and scripture to help us see. They call on the theological giants of our past—Thurman, Heschel, Tillich, and Niebuhr, to name just a few. We are served a veritable feast of words from those who have thought about justice, love, and power for us. And they bring us not only their own life experiences but also a multitude of teaching tools and group exercises that will enable us to call forth our own experiences for mutual exploration and elucidation. In this way the volume is a pedagogical gem. It is a culmination of important themes of relationality, metaphor, and systems thinking that have been integral to the authors' previous research and writings. But in other ways, it is a prelude to their research to come. That is what we hope; we want more.

In this volume we are called both to confession and to a determination to transcend the seemingly insurmountable barriers that divide us. Can we choose to be siblings by choice? Can we somehow choose to do the will, the "pleasure," of God? Can we, in a world where fear breeds violence and violence breeds fear, choose to heal the "breaches" that divide our landscapes? Can we exchange life for death? We are reminded in stark and challenging ways that we do, indeed, have a choice, that we and those who call the church home have at our disposal redemptive forces that can be unleashed on a fragmented world.

An easy task? No, certainly not. The authors never maintain that it will be. But they invite us on an adventure-filled odyssey—one in which we can see the journey's end only in brief glimpses. *Siblings by Choice* is one glimpse into a world of conversation and convergence where the ladder we are given is as high as the obstacles we are invited to transcend.

Thanks be.

Mary Donovan Turner, M.Div., M.S.S.W., Ph.D.
Pacific School of Religion
Berkeley, California

Siblings in Struggle—Siblings by Choice?

"I have cried because of hunger." "Ich habe geweint vor Hunger."
"Naan Pasiyinal Azuhiren." "Meefo Ke Homo." "Jk heb gehuild van
honger." "Ekse'gtol Sirtam." "Ila nutsin haljast." "Tenho chorafo por
causa da fome." "Tengo ihorado por la hambre." "Je crier pour la faim."

"Who are my mother and my brothers?"
"Whoever does the will of God is my brother and sister and mother."

Mark 3:33, 35

As I watch my friends, students, and colleagues dropping off around
me, I am struck by how completely vulnerable we are as humans, and
how interdependent and connected we all really are.

Janice Giteck, 21 August 1992

I

Who are my true siblings and family?

The purpose of this introductory chapter is to state the questions
that guide the book's inquiry and identify its organizing metaphor.
We explore two questions: How is it possible for women, men, and
children from different cultural and spiritual backgrounds to come
together and struggle against common forms of oppression, and in
that process become siblings by choice? How can we create

relationships of resistance, safety, holding, and trust and make connections as teachers and practitioners of pastoral care and counseling while we acknowledge and find value in differences? These are urgent questions in a world torn by war, international terrorism, religious intolerance, corporate greed, poverty and hunger, duplicity and lies. In such a world we may not have a vision of "how interdependent and connected we all really are"—our fundamental relatedness. We may not perceive that we come from a thread of common human experiences and that we need one another in order to survive or live well.

The term *sibling*, or kindred, is used metaphorically. It means belonging together, in a human family. We all have the same beginning—birth—and we all have the same end—death.[1] Between our births and deaths we need one another to create and sustain loving relationships, trust, community, meaning and purpose, food, shelter, a sense of security, and well-being. True, we are differently situated. We evolve through different cultural, economic, social, political, and personal circumstances. We are dependent on one another, the natural environment, and caring relationships to sustain the one world we share with all living things. Ideally, we may come to recognize that our diverse yet mutual interdependency weaves a richly textured and common thread of human experience. We are challenged to listen, learn, care for, and help one another in the process of maturing in the one world we share.

II

The world as we know it is changing rapidly as its population is shifting due to war, famine, drought, flooding, economic collapse, political upheaval, persecution and suffering, and technological innovations. Cultures that once appeared fixed in a geographical location are no longer stable, and societies, especially urban centers, are changing intercultural realities. What we know to be true becomes obsolete, and one's own cultural story is eclipsed by another or soon becomes one among many. Intrigue, conflict, confusion, misunderstanding, xenophobia, prejudice, and the temptation to retreat or fight are bound to arise. These dynamics of cultural change both repel and attract. We can decide whether to struggle against one another as predators and as enemies or to struggle together as siblings facing unprecedented change. The decision to struggle together we call "siblings by choice."

Definitions and concepts of family and siblings vary according to context and historical development. The term *sib* means related by blood. It generally refers to a sister or brother or to a group of people recognized by an individual or group as her or his kindred.[2] The root of the term *sibling*, sib is connected to *sippe*, meaning kin, kindred. This rendering of the term *sib* may be limiting. We explore this idea of sibling, first in the context of early Israel, and then in the context of Mark's gospel.

The idea of "siblings by choice" has roots in Israel's early history. We learn of sibling rivalries, betrayal, peace-making, and cooperation among siblings in the biblical text. Early Israel was a complex social totality called out by common responses to the vicissitudes of certain historical developments. Israel comprised different aggregates of landless people, bound together in a many-pronged struggle for a just and peaceful world. According to Prof. Norman Gottwald, there is considerable evidence that earliest Israel was formed out of disparate people with common interests amid all their differences.[3] In this light, the terms, *family, clan, household, kinship,* or *tribe* were not limited to blood relations. The term *family* had a broad application. It was applied to "an amazingly varied array of kinship and socio-political arrangements. The specific terms [family, clan, kinship, tribe, household] really only make sense in some larger analytic system."[4] The idea of siblings, then, would fit into this broad understanding of family or kinship. *Family* was a unit, a subdivision of a wider social totality, that pointed to "the peculiar identity of the community as a collectivity..." known as the people, or tribes, of Yahweh.[5]

There is precedence in the Hebrew Scriptures for the idea of siblings by choice. Terms such as *family* and *kinship* as applied to early Israel or groups within Israel appear to attest to a matter of choice. Joshua "gathered all the tribes of Israel to Shechem."(Josh. 24:1) He summoned them to "put away" the foreign gods that their ancestors had served in Egypt and turn their hearts to Yahweh (24:14, 23). He challenged them to choose which gods they would serve, if they were unwilling to serve Yahweh (24:15); "But as for me [Joshua] and my *bayrith* [household, family, clan, or tribe], we will serve the LORD" (24:15b). Joshua then leads the gathered people in renewing their covenant with Yahweh (24:23–25).

This rendering of the term *sib* may also be limiting. We turn to the words from Mark's gospel for a more expansive view. "Whoever does the will of God is my brother and sister and mother." Mark's gospel offers a unified and transcultural metaphor for our project. Siblings are not limited to blood ties or household or tribe, but are related in doing the will of God. The phrase "will of God" occurs sixteen times in the New Testament, but only once in Mark's gospel, where it appears in the plural form.[6] The Greek term for *will*, in Mark's gospel, is *thelema*. It means "desire" or "pleasure." Doing the divine will or pleasure is decisive for following Jesus. Therefore, these words "Whoever does the will of God" are addressed to those who follow Jesus, the doer of the divine will.

The gospel of Mark, according to Prof. Mary Ann Tolbert, is "an apocalyptic story, promising those presently in suffering and degradation that the much desired end is coming when all of God's enemies, human and demonic, will be defeated and the present cruel world of suffering for God's chosen will be no more."[7] It is in this context of suffering and persecution that we read Jesus' words about sibling relations and family. We are his sister, mother, brother, and members of his family when we join with him in doing the will of God. "Jesus defines his new family over against any kind of blood relations clan or tribal loyalty. The only requirement to be a member of this new family of Jesus' is to do the will of God."[8]

To follow Jesus is to move beyond thought and into action and to become a doer of the divine will. Doing the will or pleasure of God implies nonconformity with convention and openness to the new age that God is bringing about. The *New Revised Standard Version* reads: "And looking at those who sat around him, he said, 'Here are my mother and my brothers! Whoever does the will of God is my brother and sister and mother'"(Mk. 3:34–35). The *Jerusalem Bible* reads: "And looking round at those sitting in a circle about him, he said, 'Here are my mother and my brothers. Anyone who does the will of God, that person is my brother and sister and mother'" (Mk. 3:34–35, *Jerusalem Bible*). Jesus' constant openness to the will or pleasure of God places the same demand for openness on the followers. The true relatives of Jesus are not those who are physically related to him through blood ties, but *Whoever does the will of God.* Faithful performance of God's wills of healing, clothing the naked, visiting the imprisoned and infirm, feeding the hungry, and setting captives free are characteristic of those who belong to the eschatological family of God.

There is another reference to brothers and sisters and mother in Mark's gospel:

> Peter began to say to him, "Look, we have left everything and followed you." Jesus said, "Truly I tell you, there is no one who has left house or brother or sisters or mother or father or children or fields, for my sake and for the sake of the good news, who will not receive a hundredfold now in this age—houses,

brothers and sisters, mothers and children, and fields with persecutions—and in the age to come eternal life." (Mk. 10:28–30)

Following Jesus is costly. It involves decision and purpose (to spread the "good news" of God's reign), sacrifice (leave everything and follow), setting priorities, and commitment in persecution. There is the promise that when one gives up "everything"—which includes the priority of clan; tribe; blood ties to brother, sister, mother, and father—then one will find new connections again and again, a hundredfold—houses, brothers, sisters, mothers, and children in this age, and in the age to come, eternal life. "For Mark, Jesus…is the one sent by God to show everyone the way that must be followed for salvation and eternal life, a way that involves suffering persecutions, the cross, death, and then resurrection."[9]

Followers of Jesus may live in hope and continue in faithful service amidst persecution as they share his healing ministry. But following Jesus is never easy. This call to be in new sibling relationships will challenge tradition. It will mark followers as nonconformists, deviants, and put them in conflict with more limited understandings of family based on blood ties, nationalism, race, gender, sexual orientation, or class. It may come into open conflict with programs of ethnic cleansing, for example. Doing God's will is no insurance against persecution and suffering. It does not protect one from violence or misfortune. It is not a prophylactic against betrayal and estrangement. One may become fearful, faithless, or disillusioned or seek easy escape if one is looking for a guarantee against persecution and suffering. Jesus himself lives in the gap "between suffering and hope, the breakdown of the old and the promise of the new."[10] His followers failed to understand him, and in the end they deny knowing him. Disturbing is the idea that even Jesus' *siblings*—his new family—abandoned him. They ran away in fear. "Judas, his disciple and supposed brother in the family of God"[11] betrayed him. We are presented with a complex picture. Positive and negative examples of membership in the new family of God arise. Followers are called. They leave their work behind to follow Jesus. They are entrusted with God's power to do good work. The good work that challenges the members in the new family of God includes a critical engagement with religion, courage to face fear, and threats to one's life. Doing God's will, for Jesus, included the cross—that is, persecution, suffering, and physical death by the state. We are led to some critical questions: If membership in God's new family is no guarantee against suffering and persecution, then how will contemporary followers of Jesus keep hope alive in doing God's will? How will this call to a new kind of family hold them together across cultures and different faith traditions, among gender differences and in the heated controversies over different sexual orientations, amidst ethnic hatreds, and through the evils of race and class divisions? How will this call help us to choose and fully embrace siblings who live with physical and mental disabilities? Mark's gospel is relevant to these questions because of its "dramatic portrayal of [the] fateful struggle between the forces of evil and the forces of good, between the persistence of fear and the possibility of faith."[12] Mark's gospel holds out this radical call to be siblings by choice amidst present suffering and seemingly insurmountable obstacles. Its only binding cord is to do God's will. And it is a binding cord that can stretch and hold across differences—gender, race, and sexual orientation, and cultural, national, and international boundaries. This call to be family is particularly relevant for communities of the poor and others living under persecution and seeking to keep their faith alive as they remain faithful and endure in the struggle for a new heaven and a new earth.

III

Family based on blood ties and tradition would reflect the established cultural arrangements of first-century Palestine. In this context, Jesus' words are revolutionary in that they are a fundamental challenge to conventional understandings of family relations. They present a vision of humankind as fundamentally interrelated, a new integrated whole. This enlarged vision of human relatedness is lost when sibling relations are limited to blood ties and when "will of God" becomes a euphemism for exclusive or self-righteous claims.

These words, "Whoever does the will of God is my brother and sister and mother," were uttered in a world where bloodline was very important. It was a world bound by tradition, cultural divisions, and ethnic loyalties. The question, "Who are my mother and brother?" and the answer, "Whoever does the will of God," were invitations to the ancient world to rethink the meaning of family and sibling relations. They are invitations to us as well. They invite us to question conventional understandings of family and sibling relations. These words from Mark's gospel invite us to a new vision of siblings that extends to all who do God's will.

Mark's vision of siblings relates to a deeper layer of awareness. Twentieth-century mystic Howard Thurman articulates this deeper layer. He believes that there is the "scent of the eternal" in every living thing.[13] This "scent of the eternal" is the ground for the kinship of all life and our sense of a shared humanity. Thurman expresses it this way:

> It is my belief that in the Presence of God there is neither male nor female, white nor Black, Gentile nor Jew, Protestant nor Catholic, Hindu, Buddhist, nor Moslem, but a human spirit stripped to the literal substance of itself before God. Wherever man has this sense of the Eternal in his spirit, he hunts for it in his home, in his work, among his friends, in his pleasures, and in all the levels of his function. It is my simple faith that this is the kind of universe that sustains that kind of adventure, and what we see dimly now in the churning confusion and chaos of our tempestuous times will some day be the common experience of all the children of men everywhere.[14]

How can such a vision survive in a world marked by estrangement, where fear, violence and destruction, deceit and betrayal, revenge, and despair appear to reign, a world that does not know the way to peace or have a vision of how to exist in harmony with justice? In short, does this vision have a future?

Thurman believes it does. He believes in the kinship of all life, the interrelatedness of all things, and that when we are stripped to the literal substance of our being, we might discover the oneness of humankind. This is a vision hidden deep within the mystery of an unrecorded past and rooted in the primordial stirrings of the human spirit.[15]

The vision of the interrelatedness of all things resists the idea that fear, violence and destruction, betrayal and deceit, greed, and despair have final say. This vision of our shared humanity points the way to possibilities for "transcending all barriers alien to community."[16] The ideal of familial and sibling relations of care is where this sense of the eternal and self-other-consciousness first emerges. Caring acts such as love, kindness, repentance, and forgiveness are learned and practiced in the family. Such acts can make a difference and bring renewal in everyday life. But this ideal way is not apparent in persecution and suffering and in situations of deceit, oppression, injustice, violence, fear, and despair.

We chose the metaphor of sibling relations in order to develop an intergender and interethnic vision for the teaching and practice of pastoral care and counseling. This vision struggles to respect difference and make connections in a world that is often hostile to the stranger and shuns differences. In light of this sibling metaphor we explore the questions, *How is it possible for women and men from different cultural backgrounds and religious traditions to recognize, come together, and struggle against common forms of oppression? How can they become siblings by choice?*

Our guiding questions are made urgent by the forces of oppression that derive from histories of religious intolerance and conflict, international tensions, racism, class divisions, gender inequality, and violence and discrimination against those living with physical and mental disabilities. Such forces work against the recognition of our common humanity. They work against efforts to build sibling relationships of safety, holding, and trust where differences are apparent. Such forces make the achievement of human communities difficult and perhaps impossible. Caregivers struggle in the light of this challenge and in the freedom that Christ gives to work for a new kind of sibling relationship, with changed and empowered relations.

When people are thrown together by external circumstances, they may discover themselves as siblings in a common struggle against whatever it is that oppresses them. They are siblings in struggle, perhaps, but not yet siblings by conscious choice. Siblings in struggle have not yet explored spiritual resources and biographical connections that might fortify them against internal sources that can erode trust, call forth fear and hatred, create new forms of tyranny, and destroy people and movements from within. We believe there is an opportunity today for women and men struggling together to recognize that they are joined as siblings, not by happenstance nor sightlessly pitted against one another as natural enemies. They can face the forces of oppression and take a next step. They can *choose* to be siblings and spiritual allies who recognize, name, and struggle against common forms and patterns of oppression in order to achieve a better, safer world. In this way, they participate now in the eschatological family of God. Through self-conscious decision-making they can work together on those issues that divide while acknowledging that their differences represent unique ways of seeing. Their differences can provide alternative approaches to solving complex problems. Such differences can also contribute toward misunderstandings, especially where trust is lacking and narrow self-interest prevails. When people choose to be siblings across hostile divisions, they can learn and work together for the transformation of self and society and their immediate situation. Hence, it is possible to be siblings by choice, rather than siblings by default. But this path is never easy. It may be like entering a labyrinth—a maze of bewildering experiences.

We believe that spiritual experience and faith communities operate in the background and sometimes serve to contradict, and at other times provide challenge to, our taken-for-granted view of the world. We argue that patterns of gender and race relations are always already embedded in a larger complex narrative, from which specific patterns of gender and race relations emerge. The patterns that underlie our relations are often obscured and limited by prevailing interests, knowledge, and practices. Such knowledge, which often serves as an unquestioned premise for thinking and acting, needs to be made visible. To search for the origin and historical development of specific patterns of gender and race is a way to unveil certain power interests. The purposes and power interests they serve must be acknowledged.

Dominant knowledge must also be socially and spiritually located. For instance, who defines differences and common interest? How does such knowledge enable and/or limit care for one another? How does it help us to discern and do God's pleasure and enable a right or just relationship with God *and* world? It is this process of questioning conventional wisdom and practices, locating us, and uncovering historical, social, and spiritual resources that provides foundations for social and personal transformation.

In the situation of everyday life, siblings cry for hunger; that is, they cry for food, water, and nurturing relationships of justice, love, power, and freedom. This cry can be heard around the world in every culture and in every language. Homelessness, hunger, and poverty continue to be significant problems in a developed nation such as the United States—where approximately 4 million low-income children under the age of twelve experience hunger each year and an additional 9.6 million children are at risk of hunger.[17] Hunger persists in the developing countries of Asia, Africa, Latin America, and poorer countries of Eastern Europe. In many of these countries half of the people do not have access to safe water or basic sanitation. In some places—such as Afghanistan, Botswana, the Sahara, Somalia, and Rwanda—children, women, and men are dying of AIDS and are dying for lack of food, clean water, and adequate medical care. In other places, such as Guatemala during the 1970s, tens of thousands of children and men disappeared, and women were widowed, raped, and killed without redress. Siblings, often pitted against one another as informers, were hungry for the cessation of violence, wanting instead justice and healing. Their cry for hunger and the words from Mark's gospel challenge us to rethink the meaning of family and sibling relations that are based on blood ties alone. Words from Mark's gospel and a more ancient vision are invitations to become brothers and sisters and to develop nurturing sibling relations around the world. Who were the real kinfolk of Jesus? Jesus' kinfolk were those who did the will of God. Through faithful action, they continue to announce the in-breaking realm of God.

The challenge to be siblings by choice and across cultures will not be easy because we live in a world that fears differences. It is a world marked by cries of hunger, terrorism and torture, betrayal, revenge, intergenerational trauma, and ever increasing levels of domestic violence. The world at large may not know how to have cross-cultural families. More importantly, we may not have a vision for such families and a belief that they can exist in harmony. For example, few believe that Jews and Palestinians can share the ground they both claim. The world has given up on them. Separation and destruction are the models.

In the following pages we portray a complex picture that is marked by painful historical memory, duplicity and deceit, violence and need for healing and reconciliation, disappointment and promise, pain and hope, suffering and redemption. It is against such a background that we explore the significance of an intercultural sibling metaphor for the teaching and training of pastoral care and counseling. It is a metaphor about redemption amid deceit and suffering, rooted in Mark's gospel's new eschatological family of God. How is it possible for women and men and children to come together and struggle against common forms of oppression, and in that process become siblings by choice? The tools we use to explore our questions are narrative agency, systemic thinking, and intercultural realities.

IV

Narrative agency means that we are purposeful creatures, born into a particular society and culture at a particular point in its development. We act purposefully in the world by learning the language of our society and developing the capacity to cooperate. We internalize our society's values; develop a mind, an identity, and character; make moral commitments; and share a moral vision. These comprise a part of our assumptive world—an internalized set of assumptions that serve as blueprint and motive force for our actions or sense of agency. For better or worse, we are a part of the creation, maintenance, routine, and renewal of the world of everyday life. We make our contribution, grow older with others, and perhaps, if we're lucky, leave our trace. Narrative agency, then, is largely the story of our experience with others and through time, that is, how we make our way through the society and historical period in which we live.

Another way to say this: Narrative agency is the story we live as we purposefully order our lives according to certain cultural norms and values, create meaning as we pursue our dreams, and interpret ourselves in relations with others.

People may use words, gestures, and metaphors to frame and reframe, construct and deconstruct their experiences over time. They may draw on mythology and the construction of preferred knowledge to tell their personal and collective stories. Gender, race, sexual orientation, and class relations are often embedded in larger, complex narratives but have been limited by dominant knowledge and paradigms. Certain narratives from different cultures may inform the choices of women, children, and men, of gay, lesbian, transgendered, and questioning persons to struggle together and across class, ethnic, cultural, and religious differences for the transformation of society, gender relations, and the self. Hence, narrative agency is based in experience, and experience is inherently social, relational in nature. Experience is the fundamental datum of knowledge about reality. Narrative agency assumes that both *self* and *world* are woven together in the story of our lives. People tell about themselves and their environment in co-presence. Narrative thinking may be described as the many ways people bestow significance on their experiences through performance and by reflecting on them through language, belief or convictions, and activities. Narrative thinking derives from relations with others, our ancestors, the Divine Spirit, and in light of certain normative symbols that define and give shape and meaning to our thinking and living—and our world.

Systemic thinking is a way of thinking about multipersonal and reciprocal influences within certain contexts and making connections between our social location, immediate life situation, and the wider world of which we are a part. We may ask, When people from different cultures and systems of meaning meet, what happens to their beliefs and patterns of meaning making? What happens to their guiding truths, norms, and story? If their guiding story is one among many, are all stories reduced to "myth"? How can they make sense of their experiences? Systemic thinking can enable us to see the underlying patterns that connect one story with another when people from different cultures and systems of meaning meet. Systemic thinking can enable the discernment of a broader pattern of meaning. It involves recognition of a reciprocal relationship between inner self and public self, action and belief, social and cultural patterns, social worlds, past obligations, traditions, and meaning that continue to emerge from our ongoing interactions. Individuals and their relations are never static, but always negotiating, choosing, acting, emerging, and becoming in multiple contexts. Hence, in systemic thinking we track the evolution of thought and action and the newly emerging realities that arise from and are modified by the ongoing interactions people have with themselves and their environments.

Intercultural realities are the coming together of influences from many different streams of cultures and systems of meaning. We can be confused or informed and enriched by different ways of construing the world, different cultural practices and perspectives on those practices, and different ways of living in the world. We may ask, What in the world is going on, and what are the forces that are moving people around the global village? Many are being uprooted and displaced by famine, war, and violence. Some seek asylum in other countries. Others who are able to move may do so voluntarily. Societies are intercultural and transcultural realities. Their diversity will continue to increase. How do we live in a world of increased diversity with multiple realities and tensions? We will explore the influence of different international experiences, ethnicity and class, gender and religious differences, prejudice, discrimination, and segregation on practice, learning, and teaching. Our assumption is that practices such as teaching, psychotherapy, pastoral care, and counseling are culturally embedded, value laden, not neutral, and, therefore, not free of social and political ideologies and cultural bias. Intercultural realities are always a part of our one complex and interdependent world whether we recognize them or not. Therefore, intercultural realities imply an approach that takes seriously the cultural context.

In the chapters ahead, we use cases from different cultures to explore the influences of estrangement—trauma and suffering, terror and violence, deceit, betrayal and abandonment—on the call to be siblings. We will explore the obstacles to community and challenges that face people in their willingness to struggle together as siblings by choice. Narrative agency, systemic thinking, and intercultural realities are tools that shed light on our struggle. They can help us to uncover resources that point to our fundamental interrelatedness— resources that enable us to endure and to face estrangement with hope. We become siblings by choice when we struggle together to do the will or pleasure of God.

EXERCISE

In threesomes:

1. Share with other group members information about your siblings in your family of origin. How many brothers and sisters did you have? Are they living? Where do they reside? Where do you come in the birth order (for example, are you the oldest sister?)? If you were an only child, were there people close to you whom you thought of as siblings?

2. Read Mark 3:31–34 and 10:28–31. What does the phrase "will of God" mean to you?

   Write down your thoughts. What questions do you have about these two texts? What problems or challenges do they present? What do these texts say about relationships? priorities? community?

   Discuss your thoughts in your small group of three.

3. Jesus often tries to persuade the disciples to think in ways different from the prevailing ways of the world, different from the status quo. What is Jesus asking of his disciples in these two texts? What does the phrase "Whoever does the will of God is my brother and sister and mother" (Mk. 3:35) mean to you? And how do you feel about the verse "Truly I tell you, there is no one who has left house or brothers or sisters or mother or father or children or fields, for my sake and for the sake of the good news, who will not receive a hundredfold now in this age—houses, brothers and sisters, mothers and children, and fields with persecutions—and in the age to come eternal life" (Mk. 10:29). In your mind who is included or not included in the "hundredfold"?

4. What difference would it make if we considered *every* lonely, aging woman or old man we encountered as our "mother" or "father?" How would our world change? How would we?

2

Autobiographical Perspectives

Narrative Agency, Systemic Thinking, Intercultural Realities

Their lives are pieced together from swatches and shreds of many colors and patterns, as though these long-forgotten people had left patches of their clothing, their very skin sometimes, on the cruel brambles of history.

Fray Angelico Chavez[1]

But we have this treasure in clay jars, so that it may be made clear that this extraordinary power belongs to God and does not come from us.

2 Corinthians 4:7

Caring is the greatest thing, caring matters most.

Friedrich Von Hugel[2]

I

Each society constructs the self in different ways. Society greatly influences the individual, but individuals, through their ongoing interactions with others and within institutions, influence society. As we live our lives, interact with others, and journey through society, we create meaning and develop certain beliefs and ways of knowing and seeing the world around us. We develop a character and specific identities. We create stories.

When people from different societies, cultures, and systems of meaning meet, what happens to their stories, beliefs and ways of knowing, seeing, and meaning-making? What happens to their identities, guiding truths, and norms? In short, how do people from different societies and cultures find common ground? This chapter is about finding common ground. It is about how the themes of narrative agency, systemic thinking, and intercultural realities developed from the backgrounds of the authors.

The authors of this book are pastoral caregivers and teachers from different religious traditions, societies, and cultural, ethnic, and gender backgrounds. We believe that pastoral caregivers or secular therapists from different cultural, ethnic, and religious backgrounds who choose to work collaboratively across cultural divide are rare.

How can a European-born woman—who is from a Lutheran and Catholic background, a therapist and pastoral theologian, the single mother of two boys, and a White feminist—and an African American man—who is of Baptist tradition, married without children, and a family therapist and pastoral theologian—work together and find common threads in their work? How did this choice to become siblings come together in our experience?

II

It was at the Third International Conference of Pastoral Counseling in San Francisco in 1983 when we met for the first time. Important questions and directions for pastoral care and counseling emerged from that international conference. We briefly describe that setting.

The international counseling movement dealt with the importance of narrative and symbols in pastoral care and counseling. Participants from each continent were invited to present an important story of their specific cultural and religious background in order to portray their approaches to care and counseling. Archie was invited to lead a group of people who observed the process of the plenary sessions and provided feedback from diverse voices for the audience. Ursula was asked to present one of the founding myths of the European countries, found in Greek mythology in the story of the maiden Europe who was abducted from her home by the head of all gods, Zeus, in the gestalt of a bull; brought to Crete; raped; and left on her own. There was a growing recognition by the participants that the traditional models of pastoral counseling were culture bound and, therefore, limited. They were not sufficient to respond to the challenges of global development, forced removal from one's homeland, the abrogation of human rights, and cries because of hunger, terrorism, and torture especially in the so-called developing countries. There was recognition of a need to develop pastoral care and counseling models that reveal the veiled connection between personal suffering and political impotence. Models and strategies were needed to enable analysis of economic, cultural, and religious hegemony, exploitation, and human rights violations. Pastoral caregivers were challenged to fashion creative responses to violence and to develop nurturing relationship in their various contexts. The emerging challenge was to learn to see the dynamic interplay between personal suffering and the callous use of unilateral state power. How can we do this and not lose sight of the needs of individuals, families, and groups? The richness of narratives from different traditions of healing became evident and left us with the challenge to enlarge and widen the horizon of European American therapeutic and religious models and methods.

Since that international conference, we have furthered an intercultural conversation on pastoral care and counseling. We have met on other occasions and realized that even though we come from very different cultural, racial, ethnic, and religious backgrounds, our work is structured similarly. The themes we address have much in common. Both of us connect the areas of ministry, pastoral therapy, and teaching on a graduate school level. We interweave insights from indigenous experience, psychoanalytic theory, therapeutic praxis, sociology, psychology, and theology. We reflect on economic and political development and engagement. In concert with other caregivers, we are deeply concerned with the divisive impact of colonialism, race, gender, class relations, and homophobia on pastoral work in various communities. We have lived and taught in different international settings. We share with other caregivers a concern about the reproduction of colonialism; nationalism; race, gender, class, and same-sex preference stereotypes in mass media, political circles, educational institutions, and the activities of children today.

Even though we are separated by culture and miles, it has been important to stay in contact and, when possible, to work together in training, teaching, and writing. We decided to become professional siblings and strive to do so in the spirit of Mark's gospel.

In order to explain further what brought us together and still keeps challenging us, we will tell more of our stories.

Archie's family roots are in Africa; his immediate family came from a long history of oppression and exploitation in rural

Mississippi. By contrast, Ursula's ancestors were part of a well-established entrepreneurial tradition of Bohemian glass manufacturing in the Austrian-Hungarian monarchy. Archie's parents got to know each other by writing letters. They had never met in person prior to marriage. A family member sent photos from Seattle, Washington, to Natchez, Mississippi, and encouraged them to write. They did, finally meeting on their prearranged wedding day. They started a new family of five children. They stayed married until parted by the death of Archie's father. Ursula's mother married a partner who was twenty years older than she. The oldest child, a boy, was killed in combat in Russia before Ursula and her sister were born in the middle of World War II.

Archie's father stayed with his job as a city maintenance worker for more than forty years and never received promotions. Recognition and a source of pride came from serving the church as a deacon. Archie's mother took on several jobs as a domestic worker. She spent her time and energy co-raising their five children and serving as a deacon in a Black church, as a scout leader, as a teacher's aide, and as a domestic worker. These were the years of World War II, and there was much talk, fear, and concern about the war in Europe, especially Germany, and about American Japanese relations. Would Seattle be bombed, with Boeing, the airplane manufacturing company, located there? With family help and sacrifice, hard work and savings, and the encouragement of the Black church, Archie found ways to fund his education.

Ursula's parents went through the aftermath of the war and were separated for five years, leaving mother and children to the mercy of relatives. Ursula's mother worked as a secretary. After her father returned from war prison, her mother stayed at home, and they lived a secure, middle-class life in their own home. They did not experience economic hardship. Her family funded Ursula's education, and she was one of the first women to serve as a minister for eleven years in an underprivileged suburb in Hamburg.

Ursula was one of the first female pastoral counselors, trainers, and professors of practical theology in Germany. Whereas White women have been increasingly promoted in the United States and Europe during the last decades, African American scholars, women and men, still struggle for recognition in both White America and Europe. In the pastoral care and counseling movement, the voices of women and people of color have been underrepresented. Eurocentric models of care prevail. Only recently is there a growing awareness of ethnic minority presence, culture, and experiences of marginalization and the importance of these as resources for an expanded interpretation of pastoral care traditions and knowledge.

The differences between our biographies manifest themselves as different ways of communicating and working. They may suggest ways of connecting themes of personal suffering, political activity, and social transformations. Archie identifies several themes that emerge from his biography. These themes inform his work as a family therapist and pastoral caregiver. They include the creation of or search for a non-hostile environment, self-other respect as inseparable, the importance of community, acknowledgment of unmerited suffering, and the facing of rejection and humiliation with purpose and creative response. Biographic themes further include self-reliance in building up strength from within, self-trust, and a clear sense of boundaries. The working assumption is that the "White system" operates in ways that deny the worth of nonWhite ethnic minorities and their cultures, rendering them powerless and invisible. Those who are culturally in charge of the White system tend to attribute problems to individuals rather than to the system or interaction between person and system. This working assumption permits one to resist the opaque workings of the system and to search for an alternative space in which worth and esteem are possible. In an alternative space the unquestioned can be questioned; counter witness or subversive stories are created and shared; and new ways of seeing, naming, and knowing are possible. Those who share this perception and undergo such experiences can work to build networks of relational power that make social transformation a possibility.

Ursula has become aware that some of her ways of responding are linked to the traumatizing experience of the war in which her family was split and scattered all over Europe and the United States. Long-standing family traditions were diminished, reversed, or lost. Certain branches of the family have lost all connections. Others know about important events but do not see one another regularly. Ursula's life has been characterized by several moves. She has been uprooted from home, homeland, and loved ones. Over the years, she has developed a deeply felt sense of compassion for refugees and women who are uprooted and in transition for political or domestic reasons. She has a commitment to the creation of a safe space for those who have been traumatized and are looking for new spaces of social and spiritual homeland. One of the strengths derived from Ursula's biography is the motivation to bridge the gaps between class, religious background, and geographical location in marriage and between siblings and stepsiblings. Therefore, Ursula's interests as therapist and teacher are directed toward the development of bridges between workers, counselors, and teachers from diverse cultures and spiritual traditions.

Some of these connecting themes are curiosity in the ways people improvise in the face of suffering or mighty denials, the expression of compassion and justice, the willingness to be vulnerable, to take responsibility for self, and to shed and share their tears. These are important starting points for resistance, holding, trusting, and liberation. The little ways in which people are slighted, ridiculed, or otherwise dismissed and diminished need to be acknowledged. Behaviors or attitudes that many would regard as unimportant can evoke strong inner responses. As therapists, we attempt to pay close attention to emotional detail and the connection of the emotions to knowledge about the larger story of life. Archie is reminded of the words of one of his teachers, Abraham Joshua Heschel, who said that what today is considered a typical dynamic of social injustice was to the prophets of Israel a disaster for humanity.[3] In terms of sensitivity, the prophet was an octave too high. The important point here is that small behaviors are not isolated events. They are cognitive and emotional expressions, products of social interactions and connected to social convention and social patterns. Social patterns help to sustain economic and social structures. These small behaviors are important because they are the stuff of social relations, communication systems, and entrenched power arrangements. They are also the subject of therapeutic change, and they enable us to see a connection between personal suffering, political activity, or apathy.

III

These are some of the challenges to the teaching and practice of pastoral care and counseling that values intercultural realities, systemic thinking, and a narrative sibling metaphor. In this sibling relationship we choose to be spiritual allies who continue to learn from differences. The world is marked by differences that violently pit people against one another. Xenophobia, the fear and hatred of foreign peoples and things, makes an enemy of everyone and everything. A narrative, systemic, and intercultural sibling metaphor can provide teachers and practitioners of pastoral care and counseling with a different norm by enabling them to find an enlarged basis for working toward a better and transformed world. They can join with others who are differently situated, and seek to do God's will.

In these ways we became siblings by choice. We chose, where possible, to work across national and international barriers, to create relationships of resistance, safety, holding, and trust and to make connections as teachers and practitioners of pastoral care and counseling while we acknowledge and find value in differences.

Lest we forget, there are some similarities between both our countries, as well as strong differences. Both the United States and Germany have aggressively pursued strategies of genocide toward minorities and ethnic populations within their borders. In the United States, the Indigenous peoples, African Americans, Chinese Americans, and Japanese Americans have been among those treated as racial scapegoats. Gays and lesbians continue to be discriminated against, scorned, and shamed. Some, like Matthew Shepherd, have been brutally murdered. Women, children of the poor, and the homeless are among the economic scapegoats today. In Germany, it has primarily been the Jewish people and other minorities.

At the same time both countries were steeped in Western humanistic philosophies and Jewish-Christian values. Twice during the twentieth century both countries were at war with each other. Each saw the other as enemy. Millions of lives were destroyed. Both countries have experienced the rise of race-hate groups and gay and lesbian bashing within their borders. In addition, there still exist strong anti-German sentiments in the United States, and anti-American sentiments in Germany. United States television programs continue to perpetuate the stereotype of the Nazi as the typical German. Americans are portrayed as nice but superficial, not well-informed about the rest of the world, and only caring about themselves. Whether recognized or not, we are already siblings in struggle. The forces of oppression bring us together. They derive from a history of colonialism, international tensions, racism, class divisions, gender inequality, and violence. We live in these realities, and they live in us. Such forces work against the recognition of our common humanity. They work against efforts to build sibling relationships of safety, trust, and holding where differences are apparent.

The authors, born during World War II, continue to be influenced by their respective societies and by this unfolding history. This history makes emotionally painful the question, Who is my mother, my sister, my brother? The question invites us to reconsider culture-bound views of sibling relations. Mark's gospel, "doing the will of God," provides an enlarged basis for spiritual discernment, political activity, and our pastoral work. In these ways we share a commitment to struggle together and across national, gender, ethnic, cultural, and class differences for a better world. This necessitates the transformation of social and personal life. We believe this commitment to work together as siblings grew from spiritual experiences that were originally nurtured in our respective faith communities long before we ever met.

IV

How do we as teachers and pastoral caregivers come to recognize the common cry for nurturing relations in different traditions and cultures? Perhaps answers lie in the way teachers and pastoral caregivers work in diverse professional settings and collaborate with colleagues and students from very different traditions. The more the setting varies over time, the more it becomes evident that a starting point for personal and professional relationships is discovered in the intense and empathic listening to one another's life stories. Stories are embedded in specific, yet different social, political, economic, and religious contexts. They can yield rich accounts of human experience. Not without reason, narrative work is of major importance in pastoral counseling, supervision, and research. It is here that common threads and unique differences become visible. One is better able to understand another's (as well as one's own) way of living and working when stories from diverse contexts are shared. If we do not know and understand a person's preferred way of communicating and where his or her special vulnerabilities and strengths are located, patience can grow thin. Then it is hard to develop and sustain beneficial cooperation over time. When we listen to one another's stories about family background and experiences of suffering within the context of social history, the obvious differences are made clear. But so are the common threads that bind caregivers together. This was our experience.

EXERCISE

The Search for Common Ground Comes through Sharing Life Stories

1. Chose a partner. You will take turns taking down each other's story.

2. Find a private, safe, comfortable spot where there will be few intrusions.

3. Set a time limit. The desired time per session would be about one hour.

4. Decide who will go first.

5. Partner A will tell her or his "life story," indicating selected memories from childhood, adolescence, and adulthood. Note birth dates, the role and place in the family of origin, and other defining parts of life, such as relationships, falling in and out of love, transitions, turning points, beliefs, emotions, events, affirmations, significant losses or gains, religious commitments and/or change of religious affiliation, etc. You may want to organize or focus your story around a selected life theme. You may also consider the following questions: When did you first become conscious of your self as a moral being—struggling with issues of right and wrong? When did you first become conscious of yourself as a sexual being? What were the messages you received about this emerging sexual being? When did you first become conscious of yourself as a spiritual being? What were the messages you received about your emerging spirituality?

6. Partner B, respectfully and without judgment, writes the story down as fast as she or he can, and with few interruptions. Partner B does not question the story or engage in conversation with the narrator. Partner B is the scribe. Partner A is the narrator. The task is to let the narrator talk freely. Let silent moments and pauses be. You may need more than one sitting to write down the story.

7. The partners meet again to go over the story that was narrated to fill in certain gaps, and for partner A to add additional information as desired.

8. Partner B, the one who writes down the story, then prints it out and puts the date of the meeting on it. Partner B will give or send the story to partner A. In past instances, partner B mailed the story.

9. The process is reversed. The partners set a time to meet. Partner A takes down the story of partner B. Follow steps 2–8.

10. Students gather in groups of 5 to discuss and share the experiences of

   (a) Telling his or her story to someone who writes it down respectfully and without judgment;

   (b) writing down someone else's story respectfully and without judgment.

   The larger group or class meets to identify common life themes in the stories that were shared. The group's members will identify what stories or parts of stories resonated with their own life story. It will search for themes and patterns that connect one life story with another. Given what you've heard, what are some possibilities of becoming siblings by choice? The larger group will identify, as relevant, intercultural themes or patterns across cultures. How were typical experiences, such as leaving home, discovering sexual identity, experiencing illness, grieving deaths, celebrating promotions, and/or lamenting demotions handled? What customs or traditions were used? How do such themes inform the way you think about or practice "doing God's will"?

3

Transcending Barriers Alien to Community

It is time for assessing and reassessing resources in the light of the most ancient memory of the race concerning community, to hear again the clear voice of prophet and seer calling for harmony among all the children of men. At length there will begin to be talk of plans for the new city—that has never before existed on land or sea. At the center of the common life there will be strange and vaguely familiar stirrings. Some there will be whose dreams will be haunted by forgotten events in which in a moment of insight they saw a vision of a way of life transcending all barriers alien to community.

Howard Thurman[1]

There are always barriers to creating community across cultures, across nations, across religions, and across racial and ethnic divides. The contemporary social and political climate intensifies these barriers and heightens our awareness of them.

The events of September 11, 2001, marked the first national and international tragedy of the twenty-first century. Hijacked passenger planes that were used as missiles destroyed the twin towers of the World Trade Center and damaged the Pentagon. Another hijacked passenger plane, Flight 93 destined for San Francisco, was caused to crash in Pennsylvania. Americans and many around the world were stunned. The response to this tragic event was a great outpouring of shock, sympathy, humanitarian concern, and promise to get the evildoers. Understandably, Americans wanted "justice!" but in the form of revenge. Moral beliefs about right and wrong, good and bad, were clearly drawn. Americans appeared to share a sense of who the terrorists were and who were not. Our attackers were in the wrong; we were the victims; we were in the right. American civil religion was in evidence in singing "God Bless America," displaying the American flag, and increasing outward acts of American patriotism. Attendance at religious worship services was up, immediately following the events of September 11. We were engaged in a holy war, a decisive battle. The forces of Good versus Evil were engaged. It was hard to discern from the mass media the impact of this event on African Americans or other minorities within United States society. How had this tragic event affected their daily lives? An opinion piece in the *San Francisco Chronicle* reported the views of one African American man:

> As a Black man in the United States, I'm terrorized every day. Terrorized by a criminal justice system that warehouses Black men and keeps me looking over my shoulder. Terrorized by a racist corporate America that keeps my brothers and sisters from advancing beyond jobs above the level of security guard or mailroom clerk. Terrorized by legislation and court decisions aimed at keeping African Americans from ever gaining equal footing in the United States. And finally, terrorized by a president who wouldn't even consider attending a conference on racism to learn more about reconciling with the people he proposes to lead. No, September 11th's terrorist acts have not affected my daily life.[2]

Was he representative of others, or was his a lone voice crying in the wilderness of American disillusionment? Others who called attention to America's duplicity and deceit in the world community were labeled as the enemies from within, unpatriotic, or anti-American. According to some, professors on university or college campuses who spoke critically of American duplicity and deceit were blacklisted and/or dismissed from their posts.

Ursula reports that the reaction to the destruction of the World Trade Center in Europe showed a wide range of emotions, thoughts, and acts. She remembers driving through the city the next morning when the German government announced a five-minute break for commemoration. All areas of life and work were invited to participate in the commemoration. Public transportation was halted. She went to one of the churches in the suburbs where she had a meeting for supervision and found several candles burning and flowers arranged with letters of support expressing concern about the violence of destruction and self-destruction.

Questions were raised that originated in a more systemic view of the events. In which context do we understand the events? What does it mean for the highly industrialized countries if one of their actual and symbolic power points of economic influence and affluence is targeted? What is the information behind the information that we do not know about? Why were so many people surprised instead of expecting even more violence, given the desperate situation of millions of people around the globe? What must happen to the "first world" that it grasps what is going on in the lives of the majority of peoples? Many people in Europe were also taken aback by the rhetoric of revenge and the dualistic worldview expressed by the U.S. government and questioned the leaders' willingness to enter another stage of warfare by splitting the world into the axes of evil versus good. More people than ever sensed and understood that the problems people of all races, gender, and classes faced locally and globally were more complex than ever, given the grandiose developments in techniques of engineering life and death and the failure to feed and shelter all living beings in a sustainable way.

We cannot understand the events of September 11, 2001, without looking at the interweaving developments between the United States, Europe, and the predominantly Muslim countries, as well as the development of Western economy, philosophy, social-political life, and Jewish-Christian traditions. Likewise, hunger, AIDS, and military catastrophes in Africa; the economic problems and marginalization of indigenous people in South America; and the destruction of extended family systems and neighborhoods cannot be adequately addressed if we do not look at the processes of colonization by Western societies in the centuries before. What we call globalization today has roots in the building of empires of diverse origins, involving unilateral use of military, economic, and cultural power over other peoples—including religious coercion and destruction of ancient traditions of spirituality and knowledge.

Issues of trust and obstacles to becoming siblings across cultures and international borders exist in certain social processes. We say "certain social processes" because obstacles to trust cannot be explained by referring to mechanisms residing inside individuals alone. Obstacles to trust are also produced in the interactions that help constitute social life and shape individual morality.[3] After the events of September 11, 2001, and after the invasion into Iraq, the question, Whom can you trust? looms large. In a time of terror and tightening of security, we are encouraged not to trust the stranger and to be suspicious of those who are different—even within our own midst. These issues pose serious challenges and seemingly insurmountable obstacles to forming sibling relationships of trust and by choice, especially across international borders.

In times like these the following questions beg for answers: Where does one turn to anchor a moral vision? Who can you trust? How is it possible for women, men, and children from different cultural and spiritual backgrounds to come together, find grounds for trust, and struggle against oppression for a better future? Obstacles to becoming siblings across cultures must be addressed in the context of a social order in which many believe it difficult to distinguish fiction from fact, lies from truth. To address these questions in a way that keeps hope alive will require courage and a moral vision that takes account of the world community, critical questions, systemic thinking, and radical action.

Working together as siblings and in trust is visionary and a radical idea. It is visionary because it points to a way of life that seeks to challenge and transcend barriers to community. It is radical because it carries the potential to exchange a gift of life for revenge and death. If Reinhold Niebuhr is correct about the brutal character of human collective behavior, the power of self-interest, and collective egoism, then the vision of siblings working together, in trust, and across cultural boundaries encounters seemingly insurmountable obstacles.[4] Even within the same culture there are the typical dynamics of competition and emotional conflicts that one would normally expect to find in family life and close relations. Siblings across international borders would experience these and face even more challenges that can be named in terms of differences in language, worldviews, taboos and cultural experience, gender, ethnicity and social class, and so on. These differences can cause conflict when cherished beliefs and values are challenged. Differences can be perceived as threatening, and they can create a climate of fear. It is important to acknowledge the challenges and the obstacles to intercultural, international conversation.

In late September and early October 1993, Archie spoke at a conference on pastoral care and intercultural theology in Mulheim, Germany. Pastoral caregivers from the West African nations of Nigeria and Ghana, Papua New Guinea, Indonesia, India, Brazil, the United Kingdom, the Netherlands, Germany, and Eastern Europe, including Estonia and Moscow, were in attendance. The seminar topic was the economy, violence, and pastoral care. With all of the sweeping changes in Western and Eastern Europe, and since the dismantling of the Berlin Wall in 1989, economic questions had been at the center of attention. The aim of the conference was to understand how adverse economic conditions were affecting our various countries and how pastoral care providers were responding to children, women, and men affected by these adverse economic conditions. Workshops were offered on the presumption that it is not possible to think of pastoral care issues apart from the economic and political conditions that underlie social life. Many people are oppressed, exploited, and destroyed, both physically and psychically, by adverse economic conditions.

Archie led one of the workshops. The workshop invited about twenty of the international participants to present representative case studies and help the rest of us to learn by broadening our understanding of the various contexts of pastoral care. We were diverse. The workshop met for three one-and-a-half-hour sessions. At one point in the workshop presenters from different countries got into a heated discussion about what is and what is not proper pastoral care. While we appeared, on the surface, to accept the fact that we had different social locations, experiences, and worldviews, there were important disagreements on what is and what is not proper pastoral care. There was limited appreciation of the fact that our different contexts and experiences and economic conditions shaped different understandings of our work. When we moved beyond the surface level of greeting one another and moved into presenting our work, some conversations became strained, strong emotions were expressed, and a few participants dropped out of the conversation or left. Working across cultures can provoke strong negative responses and reduce trust. The outsider or stranger may appear even more strange and untrustworthy. Those of us with training and expertise in communication skills, such as pastoral care providers, may find it hard to bridge certain cultural gaps and resist becoming siblings in a common struggle when differences in worldview appear to threaten cherished beliefs and values. The differences in worldview may appear insurmountable.

These difficulties seem particularly insurmountable when there is a single, limited, or exclusive focus on one's own cultural group. Where this is the case, it will be impossible to build trust and face the complex issues of interethnic group oppression. Recently, Archie attended a conference on embracing diversity. Ethnic minority pastoral care providers were in attendance. We came from Native American, African American, Hispanic, Japanese American, Korean, Filipino American, Indian, and mixed-race backgrounds. We were articulate and gave impressive presentations regarding aspects of our own cultural heritages. We failed, however, as pastoral care providers to cross racial boundaries and address the painful issues of interethnic conflicts and violence that are a part of the challenge of providing care. One attempt to bring up interethnic tensions was met with stunned silence. It is easier to talk about diversity, eat ethnic food, and wear ethnic clothing than it is to face long-standing issues of inter- and intra-ethnic tensions. None of us addressed the inter- and intra ethnic pastoral care issues of gay, lesbian, transgendered, and questioning persons in our communities. Simply because one has been discriminated against on the basis of race, gender, class, or sexual orientation is no guarantee that the marks of discrimination and common experiences of oppression provide fertile ground for building trust or for becoming siblings by choice. These issues are threatening to many, and where this is the case, homophobia and a single-group focus can be an obstacle to building trust across cultural groups. Intercultural conversation and cooperation can be challenging, and they are not without risk. Because our understandings of "normalcy" are culturally and contextually bound, it is easy to misunderstand language and behaviors that are customary in one cultural setting but aberrant in others. It is not difficult to see that culturally bound customs and expressions of humor meant to affirm and acknowledge could, in the end, lead to misunderstanding and alienation.

A few years ago, while on sabbatical in London, England, Archie agreed to see a refugee family from Rwanda with a colleague from the U.K. The refugee family consisted of a mother and her two daughters. Both daughters, young women, had run away from their mother's home to live with their aunt. There had been a long-standing feud between mother and sister. On this occasion, the mother denounced her sister by saying, "You are not my sister!" The mother was trying to get her daughters back. The reason I was seeing the family with my U.K. colleague is because the referring party believed that we could help the family with their conflict.

We requested an interpreter to be present. The interpreter and the family were Orthodox Muslim. Members of their Mosque, fifteen women in total, accompanied them. Some were dressed in traditional clothing; others were not. Our family therapy clinic had made strides in reaching out to populations that have been marginal in order to mainstream mental health services. I knew that this would be the first time that this family would come to our agency. I wanted to make certain that they felt welcomed. The Muslim Swahili-speaking interpreter was the first to arrive. She was seated when I approached. I respectfully extended my hand and introduced myself. I noticed that she looked up at me and hesitated, then looked away and faintly shook my hand. My U.K. colleague quickly came to the door of the therapy room and said in a commanding voice, "May I speak with you?!" I came out of the room, and with hands on her hips she said, "May I respectfully suggest that you not shake hands with any of the women!!" Obviously, I had made a serious blunder. But what had I done? I had crossed a culturally prohibited gender line. Men, especially strangers, do not approach Muslim women and expect to make physical contact. I was chagrined when I realized what I had done. My gesture of hospitality was culturally inappropriate. Working cross-culturally, unwittingly, mistakes will be made. The sources of some of those mistakes will reside in deeply embedded cultural experiences—different ideas about gender, power, and conventional greeting rituals—as well as ignorance and thoughtlessness.

To work across cultural, national, racial, and ethnic lines, one must have information that can be trusted. To understand the "other" and to combat fear, one must have access to reliable and clear information. Sadly, this is difficult. These are deceptive and confusing times. It is hard to know whom we can trust and what version of reality is truthful. Arts and culture critic Steven Winn sums it up this way: "This, after all, is a culture that has come to accept and even expect skewed information at best, outright lies at worst, in everything from government to advertising to art. A generation after Watergate and Vietnam, scandals that made truth a casualty has lost their power to scandalize. We live in a society of widespread duplicity and deceit."[5]

Is it the case that the majority of United States citizens accept the idea that their public officials do not tell them the truth? If this is true, then it is hard to know who to trust and what to believe. A news report pointed to the shifting and arbitrary character of the information given to us. The writer asked, "Is there anything left that matters?"

> First, they said they wanted Bin Laden "dead or alive." But they didn't get him. So now they tell us that it doesn't matter. Our mission is greater than one man.
>
> Then they said they wanted Saddam Hussein, "dead or alive." He's apparently alive but we haven't got him yet, either. However, President Bush told reporters recently, "It doesn't matter. Our mission is greater than one man."
>
> Finally, they told us that we were invading Iraq to destroy their weapons of mass destruction. Now they say those weapons probably don't exist. Maybe never existed. Apparently that doesn't matter either.[6]

In a climate of diminishing trust, How do we discern what is truthful and what is not, what matters and what does not matter? More importantly, how can we improve and extend our moral vision so that we can see more of the world and its occupants, act resourcefully, with justice and with compassion? These questions have always been important. Today they are crucial, following the sorrow of September 11, 2001. We found ourselves in a new situation where we could not comprehend the larger world and the complex issues that engulfed us. Justice was conceived in terms of revenge and death. We were hard-pressed to understand the resentment toward the United States. A climate of widespread duplicity and deceit, diminishing trust, an inability to learn from mistakes, fear of difference, and tunnel vision or lack of capacity to understand the wider world are among the reasons why we believe that working together across international borders as siblings and in trust is visionary and a radical idea.

Duplicity and deceit are features of collective behavior and the power of self-interest. Reinhold Niebuhr reminds us that egoistic elements and vested interest are a real part of social, political, economic, and religious life. "Individuals may be moral in the sense that they are capable of preferring the advantages of others to their own and enjoy moments of self-transcendence, but this is impossible for human societies and social groups."[7] Is this true of all groups, and all individuals, all of the time? Does context matter? Do culture and intercultural realities matter in our assessment of collective and individual morality? Where does ambiguity and paradox enter our assessments? We note that individuals may also be cruel, act from narrow self-interest, and are capable of contradiction and self-deception. These obviously are the barriers to working as siblings in the building of a community across divides.

Not all efforts at working collectively for a better community are futile and inconsequential. There are organizations that have made great strides in our culture to bridge and work for the advantage of all people. One such group is the Southern Christian Leadership Conference (SCLC). It played a significant role in the mid-twentieth-century civil rights movement. It was not a group in and for itself. The SCLC envisioned, planned, and struggled for human dignity and the civil rights of Black people, and for all people. They inspired and energized countless community leaders and local activists. In this way, they were a group for others in that they worked for the transformation of the whole society and stimulated hope, trust, and commitment where despair was great. We appreciate and can be informed by Niebuhr's distinction between the morality of collectives and the morality of individuals. No group or individual is beyond destructive forms of self-interest. Nevertheless, we cannot draw a sharp and unambiguous line between collective behavior and the behaviors of individuals—because of the relational nature of selfhood, the reciprocal and co-constructed nature of human behavior, and the emerging nature of human realities.

We believe that while mistakes can be made during intercultural and international conversations and collaboration, these can be occasions for learning. Archie reflected on his reaching out to take the hand of the Orthodox Muslim woman: If I had had a colleague who had been unwilling or unable to confront my unrecognized blunder, then I would not have been able to participate in the session in a self-corrective or helpful way. I would have proceeded with certain unquestioned assumptions and not had the opportunity to learn and correct my mistake. Failure to address cultural taboos and inappropriate behavior in a timely way can be among the seemingly insurmountable barriers to effective cross-cultural work.

> By itself...breaking a taboo of this kind need not have negative effects. Indeed following rules dogmatically may cause more difficulties for the therapy than if the therapist is able to communicate his or her readiness to listen and to accept and learn about cultural differences. The therapist who shows awareness of her own cultural traditions and

constructions may in this way show more awareness of culture. Conveying that differences can be tolerated may provide more points for joining than does faking similarity.[8]

While the experiences Archie had at the international conference in Germany and at the conference on diversity were initially frustrating, it is possible that the conflict and the frustrations brought new understanding to participants about the challenges and the obstacles of the work that is set clearly before us—the work we have to do if we are serious about being siblings by choice.

Our discussion here points us toward some important questions:

- What is the meaning of establishing relationships of trust amidst diversity if we are unwilling to listen to viewpoints other than our own and unable to face the history and structural realities that underlie and continue to give rise to our conflicts?
- What can we learn about ourselves from experience? What can we learn that will enable us to witness to the gospel of Jesus Christ with humility and greater integrity in a pluralistic and interfaith world?
- What can we learn from our experience that will enhance our capacity to analyze and understand our own responses in relation to complex social processes, emerging faiths and ideologies, and the workings of institutions in a postmodern political economy?

We do not answer these questions here. In the following chapter we demonstrate how the concepts of intercultural realities, systemic thinking, and narrative agency help us to understand historical processes that still have an influence on today's problems of violence between cultures, races, genders, and religions. We will show how we engage these concepts in order to retrieve and use resources that have been limited or forgotten. Culturally competent counseling and teaching is based on the awareness of context and the reconstruction of the personal and collective history of all participants. Knowledge of open and secret atrocities, wounds and traumatizations, sources of life energy, and love are crucial resources for people to gain a sense of belonging, self-agency, and healing.

EXERCISE

If Reinhold Niebuhr is correct about the brutal character of human collective behavior, the power of self-interest, and collective egoism, then the vision of siblings working together in trust and across cultural boundaries encounters seemingly insurmountable obstacles. Perhaps one of those obstacles is the difficulty of finding a moral vision and a spirituality to sustain our commitments to one another in a world of changing beliefs and morality.

1. Write about your spiritual philosophy. What does the word *spirituality* mean to you?

2. Write about spiritual paths you have explored.

3. Describe what it is that you do to keep spiritually alive during times of social unrest and uncertainty, or personal confusion, or dwindling interest in commitments to social justice.

4. Meet with two other classmates to discuss your spiritual philosophy and how you draw strength from it. What are some of your spiritual resources and practices?

5. As a threesome, discuss possible ways to support one another and to support those who may be from a different national or cultural group or sexual orientation. What might be some obstacles to connecting spiritually with others across cultural differences? In short, how might your spiritual values connect you with others?

4

Moral Vision in a Climate of Diminishing Trust

"Lies, lies, and more damn lies"

In a climate of diminishing trust, how do we discern what is truthful and what is not, what matters and what does not matter? More importantly, how can we improve and extend our moral vision so that we can see more of the world and its occupants, act resourcefully, with justice and with compassion? These questions have always been important. They are urgent questions whenever we operate, unwittingly, from tunnel vision and cannot comprehend the complex issues in the larger and changing world that engulf us.

In this chapter we present two examples of the way narrative agency, systemic thinking, and intercultural realities can come together to inform a moral vision. These can have an influence on the way we view today's problems of violence within and between cultures, races, genders, and religions. The first is an example from the movie *Kandahar*.[1] The second is from Germany.

Case Study 1

Kandahar is a movie, a documentary-drama about a journey to the heartland of Afghanistan. Director Mohsen Makhmalbaf is Iranian. He seeks to depict life under the Taliban. The movie, inspired by a true story, begins with a desire to save a life. It features the journey of an Afghan Canadian journalist, Nelofer Pazira, or "Nafas," who travels from the Iranian border toward Kandahar to find and rescue her sister who has vowed to kill herself before the eclipse of the millennium.

Nafas's sister's desire to kill herself draws attention to the extreme oppression of women under Taliban law. Temperature in the city of Kandahar has been described as oven-hot. The women who venture outside of their homes must be covered from head to toe in this suffocating heat. Their oppression is symbolized, in part, by the dress they are forced to wear. Afghan women "cannot leave their homes unaccompanied for fear of execution and…women who once worked as doctors and teachers are reduced to the daily humiliation of the Burka, the only everyday clothing ever designed as a walking prison."[2] Pazira, a practicing Muslim, lifted up her burka in defiance one day and "felt the intense stares of the people around her, and quickly covered herself." She said, "I realized what a psychologically damaging thing it is, because it makes you feel incompetent. You lose your self-confidence. And you don't have to think about your identity anymore."[3] Nafas encounters many situations of humiliation along the way toward Kandahar.

The movie *Kandahar* is complex. There are layers of stories, or stories within the story, about the journey to Kandahar. There is the story of the class of little boys being taught by the village mullah to cite the Koran from rote memory and use the sword and the Kalashnikov (an assault rifle) against the enemies of Islam—without understanding the Koran. There is the story of land mine victims who journey to the Red Cross for prosthetic legs, and the story of an old Afghan refugee and his family who are robbed by desert thieves and left to travel through the scorching desert sand on foot. There is the story of a young boy, Khak, who is expelled from a religious school and serves briefly as Nafas's guide. He seeks opportunities to exploit and deceive her. There is the story of an armed man in the road who might be a member of the Taliban or a bandit, and the story of an African American convert to Islam. I will focus briefly on Nafas' encounter with the Black American convert to Islam because of its potential to illuminate the challenges of finding trusting and caring sibling relations across international borders.

Nafas first meets the Black American in the guise of a village medical doctor who shows genuine concern for her health and her identity as a woman. After he discloses his identity to her, he recommends that she dismiss the young boy, Khak, who had promised to take her to Kandahar. Hassan Tandai surmises that the young boy cannot be trusted. He offers to take her toward Kandahar on a horse-drawn cart. On the journey toward Kandahar, Nafas learns more about her Black American guide. She speaks:

"Why did you leave the U.S.?"

"In search of God," he said.

"Did you find him?"

"No!" he said.

"So, why did you stay?"

"I'm still searching for God."

This young Black American convert to Islam is disillusioned with the mujahideen (Islamic guerrilla fighters who wage jihad [holy war] against the enemies of Islam), but he has not given up on his search for God. She speaks again:

"What medical school did you go to?"

"I'm not a *medical* doctor. I came here to fight [in the holy war]."

He had thought that the path to God was fighting against the Russians who were fighting Afghanistan (1979–1989). When Afghanistan won, the internal fighting about God began. One group of Afghans (Pashtun) said, "God is with us." The other group of Afghans (Tadjik) said, "God is with us." He fought first with one group against the other. Then he joined the other group and fought against his former comrades.

In what was his moral vision anchored?
Where was God in all of this?
And what was the distant goal?
He pondered all these critical questions.

One day, as he was traveling, he found two children, very sick, lying on the road. They were about to die. Both were Afghans; one was Pashtun, and the other was Tadjik. This Black American convert to Islam says to Nafas, "I understood [in that moment] that the search for God was in helping these people [both sides] to heal their pains."[4]

I selected the film *Kandahar* because it was released when the United States was engaged in a war with Afghanistan. Many Americans viewed the war as "us against them." The aim was to diminish the threat of terrorism by waging war on the Taliban and to destroy one man in particular. I knew little of Afghanistan. I wondered if the struggle for freedom and self-determination in that Islamic country had any relevance for African Americans. Was there something in the collective narrative of African Americans—our struggle for freedom and full humanity—that would link us to the freedom struggles of the Afghans? What can we learn about our responsibilities and role in the global community when we think about the common structure of human oppression and the struggles for freedom of an oppressed people in another country? Or is this none of our business? When I learned of Hassan Tandai's role in the film and his search for God and a guiding moral vision, my interest was piqued.

If it is true that we are fundamentally and inescapably relational beings, then we have responsibilities toward the strangers who help constitute the one planet we share. We are relational beings. Sociality, or the relational web, is key to human survival and well-being. This is a fundamental truth for all people. No one, and no society, is a self-contained, self-sufficient island unto her or himself. The thesis of the relational self is crucial for a moral vision about trust, care, and human survival. It is an important awareness for pastoral care providers. The thesis of the relational self gives us an uncommon vantage point for interpreting the pastoral care situation of help seekers. "Much of present-day pastoral care involves helping people resolve intra psychic conflict and find personal integration. As care givers, we seek to understand the conflicts from *inside* the care-seeker's cognitive world."[5] This is an important emphasis, but it may be too limited a basis for anchoring trust and assessing a moral vision for human care, survival, and well-being. As our experiences unfold within the contexts of immediate relationships, they are also guided by certain cultural norms and practices of which we are scarcely aware. Pastoral care providers are encouraged to be aware of the wider contexts that define us and help to influence the intersubjective processes that lie behind our activities. This is where our guiding concepts of narrative agency, systemic thinking, and intercultural realities come in.

Narrative agency: We live within layer upon layer of stories. We are born into a world that has already been hewed-out by lived experience and given meaning by our predecessors. We contribute our own meanings to the flow of experience, and our bestowed meanings are influenced, modified, and changed through interactions with the many others who share our world. The complex stories of our lives are "like thin layers of paint applied to a canvas, one color on top of another. Blue plus yellow equals green. Or does it?"[6] The meanings of our lives are not immediately known or assessable. We always need others to help us with the interpretation of meaning.

The stories of our lives are interwoven with the unfolding story of our society and the culture in which we are embedded. Martin Luther King Jr. would say, we are caught in a "single garment of destiny." In this light, narrative agency means that one is moved along by the deep currents of history that flow beneath the surface of society, by immediate forces, by the meanings we co-construct with others, and by the choices we make from the limited career paths that are available. One is moved along by the logic, contradictions, and unanticipated consequences of the complex, multilayered, and unfolding story in which people find themselves.

When the Black Muslim convert left the United States for Afghanistan, the story of his life would unfold in ways he could never predict. He went as a liberation fighter to help free the Afghans from Soviet occupation. Once that was accomplished, his life took a different turn when the internal struggle for power continued. His own personal quests for God led him to fight with one side of the internal conflict, but this did not fully satisfy him. Then he fought with the other side. This, also, was not fully satisfying. Perhaps he discovered that the perspective from each side was too limited. Pushed forward by his search for God, he had experiences that led him to a broader understanding of his religious quest, which was a quest for wholeness.

Systemic thinking is about making connections between events in an attempt to see a larger whole and a broader vision, and to gain a comprehensive understanding of justice. Systemic thinking would encourage us to see the complexity of oppression and to see the oppression that lives within oppression. For example, Hassan Tantai may not have seen or understood the dynamics of oppression between the Pashtun and Tadjik peoples until he was able to think about the complexities of oppression within a broader view of culture and wider view of justice. To be a worker for justice and a justice maker, you have to be a systemic thinker in order to see the complexity of injustice and the oppression on all sides.

Intercultural realities: The film does not give us information about Hassan Tantai's relationship to his group, the mujahideen. We imagine that when the Black Muslim convert arrived in Afghanistan for the first time, he underwent a long process of acknowledging and distancing himself from certain unquestioned assumptions that were a natural part of his daily life in the United States. We assume that he had to be acclimated to local customs and traditions of his new social and cultural situation in Afghanistan, and that he had to earn the trust of the mujahideen. We imagine that it did not come automatically or effortlessly. We further assume that the move from one society to a vastly different one is, at best, difficult. In this light, "intercultural" means the developing capacity over time to gain trust and engage in effective communication between members of different ethnic groups. One may always remain a stranger or be considered an outsider, but even as an outsider, one can develop the capacity to understand and communicate. Examples of this developing capacity were demonstrated in the exchanges between Hassan and the villagers as he addressed some of the health needs of the people who came to him. He said that many of the diseases that cause illness among the poor in Afghanistan can be treated from knowledge that is common among most Americans—how to treat dysentery, the common cold, an upset stomach, and certain other infections. He understood Nafas's urgent desire to go to Kandahar and the dangers involved. He offers her a handgun, but she refuses. He assesses her lack of safety in the hands of the young boy, Khak, and devises a plan with Nafas should they be stopped and questioned by a member of the Taliban while traveling together in the horse-drawn cart. He wore a false beard that he removed and glued back on as needed. Perhaps this was his version of the burka. Although he showed his unbearded face to Nafas, he could not afford to do so in the rest of his immediate world. The Black Muslim convert developed a broad experiential and intercultural narrative from which to operate. His developing intercultural narrative was one not trapped in internecine struggles between warring ethnic groups. It had the capacity to transcend them. What we surmise is that his moral vision was broad enough to hold together the children who were on different sides of their country's internal conflict. Intercultural realities were being enlarged by the very context in which his life was unfolding.

Narrative agency, systemic thinking, and intercultural realities are perspectives that mutually inform each other. They contribute to an idea of God as the One who enables us to hear a call to community through the churning confusion and chaos that would engulf us. For the Black Muslim convert, the distant goal was to fulfill a moral vision of a way of life that transcends all barriers alien to community. In the midst of struggle, his own moral vision was challenged and changed in the context of collective struggle. He was able to rethink his priorities in his search for God that carried him through times of danger and disillusionment.

Case Study 2

Mrs. M. called and complained to Ursula about her youngest child, L., who was fifteen. He no longer went to school regularly. He did not get up before noon. He looked tired and exhausted. He often yelled at his mother and was very aggressive. His mother knew that he used an illegal substance, marijuana. The teachers and school administrators were upset with him. His progress was endangered.

Ursula knew Mrs. M. from an encounter a year before this phone call. At that time, a physician called Ursula and asked if she could assist one of his clients. Mrs. M. was afraid her daughter would kill herself. The daughter was Mrs. M.'s eldest child, a young woman of twenty-three. She had been treated in a clinic for depression two years before and had been seeing a therapist on and off since then. Now she was expressing suicidal ideas.

Ursula offered her an appointment together with her daughter. The family called back and announced that the daughter, A., wanted to bring her father to the meeting. Ursula was happy that the father was willing to come. She also invited a colleague as co-therapist so they could work as a reflecting team. The session was a success in that the focus was on the communication between the parents. They worked out some important issues involving time, commitment, and anger between husband and wife. The daughter expressed great relief that she could tell her mother not to use her as a partner for the problems between mother and father. The father was out of the home often and worked a lot. Thus, the daughter was able to return some of the responsibility of the grown-ups to the parents and create space for her own life.

What was the problem with this family, a well-off, middle-class, and White Saxonian family of five? This was a family in which communication was apparently open, both parents were engaged with the family, and no severe stress was visible. Why, a year later, did the youngest son develop symptoms of drug addiction that made mother, father, and school extremely nervous? Why was it that the older son, T., had problems with his parents and regularly smoked marijuana?

The symptoms of the young adults in this family became more understandable when the whole family was invited to a workshop. The two supervisor/therapists of the family and a drug therapist offered the workshop. They saw the parents and their three young adults for two-and-a-half hours. After listening to the young people and the parents, the therapists asked the younger generation if they wanted to stay for genogram work or leave the room for a while and have their own time. They decided to leave and be called back in by cell phone later.

The next step was to develop an understanding of the generations. This included Mr. and Mrs. M. and their parents and grandparents. While working through this step it became obvious that the patterns of both families played a big role in the present situation. The husband was work-oriented, outside the house, and centered on his own needs and joys. The wife, by contrast, was more responsible for the children and household, more depressed, and angered.

Moreover, the history and political changes that both sides of the family had to experience during World War I and after had an enormous impact on the generations. The effects of the atrocities of World War II, in which Mr. M.'s father was involved, and the time of the German Democratic Republic, which shaped the youth of Mrs. M. and Mr. M., were obvious. Mr. M. had learned to repress problems and develop a career, while Mrs. M carried most of the burden at home. Her underlying depression, anger, and sadness had an impact on the children. They internalized unspoken messages of trauma across the generations.

The therapeutic strategy centered on family reconstruction. The therapists did grief and reconciling work with the parents and their parents. This allowed the younger generation to do their own work of growing up instead of caring for the grownups.

Narrative Agency through the Transmission of Intergenerational Trauma

We saw that in the family of Mr. and Mrs. M., the problems of depression, illegal drug use and abuse, and suicide ideation could be traced back over several generations. A sense of narrative agency, then, was located in certain family patterns and unconscious processes. The German psychoanalysts who worked with victims of the Holocaust over two or three generations have documented the overwhelming experiences of severe trauma on parents, their children, and their grandchildren. The grandchildren, for example, developed symptoms of psychosomatic problems such as mental illness, drug addictions, and problems around their search for an acceptable identity. Such problems were related to the unspoken legacy of their grandparents' generation.[7] The therapists noted, from this case, that a moral vision is never independent of personal identity, mental health, and family loyalty issues.

Several concepts have been developed in psychoanalytic theory and family therapy to help understand how narrative agency is transmitted through the generations.[8] The Hungarian therapist Ivan Boszormenyi-Nagy gives us one of those concepts, the *family ledger*. He assumes a kind of bookkeeping in larger family systems and relates this to a sense of justice in families where debts and balances are transferred from one generation to the next. "We regard justice as a multipersonal homeostatic principle with equitable reciprocity as its ideal goal."[9] He refers to the family ledger as "the multigenerational network of obligations (where one) becomes accountable to the chain of past obligations, traditions, etc. One may not readily be aware of the long-range *quid pro quo* moves only of short-term obligations and repayments. The less (one) is aware of the invisible obligations accumulated in the past, for instance, by (one's) parents, the more (one) will be at the mercy of these invisible forces."[10] Loyalty to overt and covert expectations in regard to justice is an important motivation for sisters and brothers in their lives.

The psychoanalytic group of Massing, Reich, and others identify other concepts where the grandparents' unresolved problems are transferred through the conscience and superego of the parents to their grandchildren. They state that the disorders and conflicts of the generation of children are regularly rooted in unconscious conflicts between parents and grandparents "and, that in families basically the same conflicts are re-enacted across the generations. There is an intrafamily compulsiveness of reiteration or repetition."[11] Those processes are mostly unconscious; therefore, it is important to address them in therapy or counseling. Here, narrative agency becomes important. Many grandchildren have no idea what their problems are about because in many families the experiences are no longer shared across generations. This factor is especially significant for cases of perpetration, violence, or collaboration of violence. This is significant for victims of trauma. Often, the truth of what happened is hidden because women and men find it too painful to remember, to feel fear, sadness, and anger. They feel shame, believing that what happened to them was their responsibility. Reconstructing the personal life story and the political context of the generation's experiences has become a crucial point in therapy and counseling. Many women pastors in Germany participate in conferences and share their stories. Younger women learn from older women who are talking, for the first time, about their experiences of being raped during World War II.

Systemic Thinking

Systemic thinking assesses the reciprocal influences of the history of drug manufacturing, the traumas of war, and the family's "invisible loyalties," responses, or coping patterns over time. Stachowske and other family therapists have shown that effective treatment of drug addiction in today's society cannot be successful without employing a systemic, transgenerational perspective and working through the personal and collective history of the victims and perpetrators of economic or military power.

The German social worker and family therapist Ruthard Stachowske did research by visiting the archives of major companies in Germany that have produced drugs since the mid-nineteenth century. He reconstructed the genograms of many families in his clinical work, read governmental reports on drug conferences around 1900, and read literature on drug developments in the U.S., Europe, and Asia. He found that the history of the development of artificial drugs in Europe (morphine, cocaine, heroin, etc.) is mirrored in the kinds of drugs used by families over the generations.

Merck in Germany accomplished the first artificial production of drugs. Merck owned a small drugstore. After his invention, he enlarged his work and developed the first industrialized production of morphine, cocaine, heroin, and the like. Stachowske's research showed that in the middle of the nineteenth century, more drugs were produced by this and other companies than were needed for medical use. The surplus drugs were sold throughout Europe and the rest of the world. A profitable industry was born. Before the first opium conferences in the early part of the twentieth century, there was access to drugs from drug companies themselves. Drugs were also available in drug stores.

Drug addiction followed the invention of the industrial production of drugs. Drugs used in families produced addiction over several generations. One famous example is the family of Charlie Chaplin. Drug use by him and his wife can be traced back for several generations. The value of systemic thinking is to view our issues within the context of wider influences and to make connections between personal and social worlds. This is illustrated in the following vignette.

Mrs. M.'s call to the therapist brings the context of her immediate problems into a system of help. Her son is acting out at school as well as at home. The school's response is to be "upset." The daughter is in danger of killing herself. How can their issues, which may be seen as unrelated or isolated behaviors, be brought together so that their reciprocal influences may be observed and understood in a wider context? We note that the son's problems were seen as home and school related. The daughter's problems were treated in a clinic. Who was working with the family, school, and clinic together?

The challenge for the help provider is to ask how these family issues are interrelated and how they are related to a larger context. The daughter, interestingly, opens an important door when she expresses the desire to have her father present for the counseling sessions. It would be important to engage the entire family and to work with a team who could work with this family and the institutions whose resources hold relevance for the family. It is important to engage the school where the son is enrolled, the clinic where the daughter has been involved, and others who are relevant to the case. This includes members of the extended family, who may prove to be invaluable. We do not know, from the information, if there is a faith community or not. If so, then how might their resources be tapped? The immediate goal is to clarify boundaries between the generations and bring stability to the family, and to identify the support they need to take for the next steps.

There is another level, that of policy and engagement of government, social, and educational institutions. We do not have much information from the case material to identify how this might unfold. How might information about drug and intergenerational influences be brought together and funded? How might research contribute to training and treatment programs funded by governmental institutions? How might families at risk or in trouble be a part of the treatment and training programs, and therefore a part of the solution? This may be a way to extend a moral vision for appropriate help.

Intercultural Realities

Ruthard Stachowske has recently published a dissertation in which he portrays new concepts of working with severe drug addicts, mostly young women, men, and their children.[12] He elicited the stories of family members from different cultural backgrounds and across the generations. Here, we note that "intercultural realities" may include a changing drug culture that evolves over time, from one generation to the next, resulting from the changing conditions of the host society. Stachowske heard from his respondents that they experienced loss, illness, breakups, or death not only within their own lives but also in the lives of their siblings and cousins, and in the previous generations. All these families were involved across several generations in historical political processes of extreme violence and traumatization by war, terrorism, or political power— for example, World War I, World War II, the Civil War in Spain, and wars between Afghanistan and the Soviet Union and between Tschetschenien and Russia. Stachowske confirms the insights of others that the grandchildren often carry, unconsciously, unresolved pain or guilt that overburdens them and leaves them in confusion.

He and his team engaged their clients in extensive work of memory across several generations by teaching them to construct their own genograms, including biographical data over several generations, historical events, economic and political situations, belief systems, and life conditions. Grandparents, if they were alive, were invited to therapy sessions in order to help their grandchildren. They seldom declined. Stachowske also visited with the help-seeker in their homes.

In these situations a moral vision was extended with resourceful acts of justice and compassion. Each case showed a way from tunnel vision to engagement with the surrounding world.

In the following chapter we further demonstrate how the concepts of intercultural realities, systemic thinking, and narrative agency help to understand historical processes that still have an influence on today's problems of violence between cultures, races, genders, and religions. We will show how we engage these concepts in order to retrieve and use resources that have been limited or forgotten. Culturally competent counseling and teaching is based on the awareness of context and the reconstruction of the personal and collective history of all participants. Knowledge of open and secret atrocities, wounds, and traumatizations must be explored. Love and forgiveness and sources of life energy become crucial resources for people to gain a sense of belonging, self-agency, and healing.

EXERCISE

If you remove the yoke from among you...
Your ancient ruins shall be rebuilt;
you shall raise up the foundations of many generations;
you shall be called the repairer of the breach,
the restorer of streets to live in.

(Isaiah 58: 9b, 12)

What can we learn about "doing God's will" and our responsibilities and role as siblings by choice in the global community when we think about the common structure of human oppression and the struggles for freedom of an oppressed people in another country?

1. Write out your reflections to the above question in light of the passage from Isaiah 58. Imagine that you are a part of a community that is known as "the repairer of the breach." What difference would that designation, "repairer of the breach," make in the way you take on responsibilities and live your life? What would you be doing that you are not doing now? How would this designation challenge your understanding of pastoral care?

2. Discuss your ideas with a class member—one that you do not yet know well or only have few opportunities to talk with. Together, identify resources from your different social locations that might enlarge your awareness of the common structure of human oppression and the freedom struggles of oppressed people, both here and abroad. Given your conversations, what would be the challenges for becoming siblings by choice? What might be some intercultural realities that could challenge your choice? How could systemic thinking help? Write down new learning or challenges.

5

Invisible Forces Determining Human Existence

> You have to engage the past if you are going to share a future that reflects you.
>
> *John Henrik Clarke[1]*

I

Have you ever felt that forces were moving you far beyond your control? The aim of this chapter is to show the connection between a historical event, such as the Middle Passage, and contemporary pastoral care.

Our thesis, simply put, is this: *The Middle Passage was a horrific event that unfolded over a four-hundred-year period. The effects are still with us—invisible, yet helping to determine human existence.* What challenges might this historical event pose for scholarship, teaching, ministry, training, and the pastoral care of souls? And what are the consequences for pastoral care, pastoral theology, and theory when a historical event on the magnitude of the Middle Passage is absent from theory and everyday awareness? What role can historical consciousness play in the constitution of the human subject, and what does it mean to live without historical consciousness? In short, if human existence is historical existence, then what is pastoral care's subject?

First, we will talk about pastoral care and suggest the role of scholarship. Second, we will talk about the relevance of historical consciousness in general. Third, we will elaborate specifically on the damaging effects of the Middle Passage as historical event. Fourth, we will present three vignettes illustrating these damaging effects. Finally, we will briefly discuss how pastoral care as a historically situated and aware discipline can address problems such as those illustrated in the vignettes. Narrative agency, systemic thinking, and intercultural realities will be addressed.

II

Pastoral Care's Incomplete Picture

There are many traditions and definitions of pastoral care in Buddhism, Islam, Judaism, and Christianity. In this light, the broad history of pastoral care is largely unwritten, unclaimed, and unknown. What may be said is that any definition of pastoral care has at its core a way of understanding historical existence; our relatedness to the higher Self, the Divine; and corresponding activity that seeks the well-being of others.

Contemporary pastoral care as a twentieth-century movement in the United States emerged primarily under the tutelage of modern psychology. It also "attempted to refine ministry by drawing upon the findings of modern medicine, psychotherapy, and the behavioral sciences."[2] In recent times, however, there have been attempts by pastoral care theologians to reclaim the discipline's theological roots as it considers such perennial concerns as sexual orientation, illness, death, family conflict, depression, divorce, and a host of complex moral and ethical questions. Today, most of the major theological seminaries across the United States have appointed full-time faculty in pastoral care, and a substantial body of research literature has appeared. Still, the contributions by women to pastoral care and those from Buddhism; Islamic traditions; Asians; Blacks, Hispanics; Native Americans; and gay, lesbian, transgendered, and questioning persons have yet to emerge as something more than mere footnotes for the discipline. These suppressed experiences and traditions with their distinctive histories have yet to make their impact on the discipline of pastoral care. Perhaps that is a challenge for the twenty-first century.

Our task, as scholars, teachers, and preachers, is to ground our understanding of the present in the rich experiences and germinal thought of our collective past.[3] This task can be shared by all of us.

What has been missing from mainstream pastoral care, with few exceptions, is a serious engagement with the critical role of historical and social analysis. The emerging voices of feminist pastoral theologians are new and important exceptions. The voices of gay, lesbian, questioning, and transgendered persons are just beginning to be heard. Without their voices our understanding of human nature is shallow, historical perspective ill-informed, and social analysis inadequate. Pastoral care is a social practice, and as a social practice it conveys certain ideologies, dominant values, and interests. And it must be evaluated as part of the evolving history, culture, and ethos of the society that shapes it.

Again, the point of this chapter is to show a connection between a historical event such as the Middle Passage and contemporary pastoral care. We will share why we think collective suffering and invisible forces help to determine human existence. We hope to offer a challenge to an entrenched paradigm that still controls definitions of pastoral care and pastoral theology. That paradigm suggests that the lone individual and the problems she or he presents can be adequately understood by identifying the underlying pathology that presumably resides in the individual and can be adequately analyzed apart from culture, historical perspectives, and social analysis. In such a perspective, the truncated individual becomes pastoral care's subject.

True, there is growing evidence to suggest that some pastoral caregivers have moved away from an individualistic model of care to one that emphasizes the *relationship between* people. A Lilly-funded project called *The Religion, Culture and Family Project,* located at the University of Chicago, recently published its research. Based on a national survey of 1,035 marital and family therapists (including a roughly even mix of psychologists, psychiatrists, social workers, and pastoral counselors), the article is the first empirical study of the ethics of what therapists actually believe and practice. They found that the majority of therapists interviewed have moved away from viewing individual needs and rights as the central focus of moral life and toward valuing the quality of persons' relations to one another. Even here, there is a strong tendency to view family relations narrowly, and frequently to the exclusion of social and cultural analysis and historical influences.

Our charge is this: Mainstream pastoral care, with few exceptions, has ignored the important role of American and European history and has helped to further an impoverished understanding of the human person and the social histories that shape us.

This leads us to other important questions:

1. How do we engage *systemic thinking*—that is, how do we learn to make connections between historical events, social analysis, and contemporary pastoral care in order to give more adequate, richer descriptions and better accounts of our world?
2. How do we engage *narrative agency*—that is, how do we develop moral vision and learn to take responsibility for self and others as siblings in our world?
3. How do we engage *intercultural realities*—that is, how do we learn to acknowledge the unequal parts of privilege and oppression that make up all positions?[4]

Systemic Thinking

What role can historical consciousness play in the constitution of the human subject? If human existence is historical existence, then what is pastoral care's focus? Is it **social worlds?** Social worlds may be the physical environment that makes up worship place, play, the workplace, neighborhood, or home. The physical environment represents the organized visible structures that we can observe. They constrain our behavior or direct our interactions in one way or another. Certain interactions may represent the history of social relations in a particular place or society over time. Certain relations between the members of society are purposefully arranged and may result in the material benefits of some, but not others.

There is another dimension to social worlds, which I call "invisible forces." "Invisible forces" operate outside of our awareness. They are the unseen and often unrecognized dynamic forces that operate indirectly behind the backs of individuals and institutions. They represent the complex, inner dimensions of the visible world. The term *invisible forces* is intended to make room for the operation of nonrational, unrecognized, immaterial forces in the life-world that influence and even help to determine human outcomes. This is to say that not everything that happens in our world emerges from awareness and can be observed, contained, or controlled by reason or by self-regulating systems.

At the heart of this presentation are a historical event, the Middle Passage, and its continuing invisible effects. The Middle Passage as an "invisible force" moves beyond our control. Such invisible forces and continuing effects are carried in social patterns, the minute details and routine of everyday life. They become much like second nature. In this sense, we do not always know all that we are doing; and much of what we do is unquestioned, embedded in tradition and convention. Systemic thinking, then, implies a connection between the visible and invisible forces that help determine human existence.

The term *habitus* comes closest to what I intend to express about the operation of the invisible powers and damaging effects. *Habitus* refers to the conventional ways of doing things that mediates between individuals, the structures of everyday life, and the wider culture. Pierre Boudieu refers to *habitus* as a system of durable and transposable dispositions.[5] It serves, in varying degrees, as a culturally encoded and largely unquestioned way of being in the world that enables individuals to cooperate and cope with unforeseen and ever-changing situations.[6] In short, *habitus* is a product of history and historical existence. It becomes a kind of second nature and a matter of routine. It produces and is produced by interpersonal power arrangements and collective practices that conform to the schemes engendered by history. It functions as the unquestioned and taken-for-granted way of being, seeing, and acting in the world.

Suman Fernando, a British psychiatrist originally from Sri Lanka, provides an illustration. He argues that psychiatry evolved as an ethnocentric body of knowledge. Because psychiatry developed in a Western culture with a strong ideology of racism, it is hardly surprising that racism has seeped into or, more correctly, been actively absorbed into the theory and practice of the discipline and become integrated into its institutional practices.[7] Over time, institutionalized practices, as mentioned above, are internalized and contribute to uncontrollable levels of stress that affect individuals, families, and communities. Consequently, people turn on each other to vent their anger, rage, hate, despair, helplessness, and hopelessness. African American men, women, and children may be caught up in damaging cycles of violent behaviors and victimization and consequently are becoming an endangered species.[8] *Habitus* is the name for this routine, unquestioned, and taken-for-granted way of being in the world. It ir worldview, attitudes, beliefs, and values, which, le, are embodied in our stock of knowledge, theory and isions, and polities. Given this, systemic thinking in the nt analysis of social worlds ought to be a part of pastoral

Intercultural Realities

On July 3, 1999, a monument was lowered to the floor of the Atlantic Ocean from the *Regina Chaterina*, a tall ship built in 1915. This act of lowering a monument to the floor of the Atlantic was the symbolic water burial of the Middle Passage. It commemorated the estimated millions of African people who died and were thrown overboard while being transported as human cargo in chains from West Africa to the Americas. Someone said, "The floor of the Atlantic is sown with the bones of my people!…[I]f the Atlantic Ocean were to dry up today, there would be a trail of human bones stretching from Africa to the Americas."

The Middle Passage, sometimes referred to as "the crossing of the waters," was the name given to that part of the Atlantic slave trade that brought the brutally captured and inhumanly treated Africans from West Africa to North America, South America, and the Caribbean. It was called a triangular trade system because "the ships embarked from European ports, stopped in Africa to gather captives, after which they set out for the New World to deliver their human cargo, and then returned to the port of origin."[9] It lasted for nearly four centuries.

Historian John Henrik Clarke writes, "Millions of African men, women, and children were savagely torn from their homeland, herded into ships, and dispersed all over the so-called New World."[10] It is estimated that only about a third of the thirty to sixty million Africans captured actually survived the water crossing.[11]

African American historian Lerone Bennett, Jr., describes the horrific conditions:

> They were packed like books on shelves into holds, which in some instances were no higher than eighteen inches. "They had not so much room," one captain said, "as a man in his coffin, either in length or breadth. It was impossible for them to turn or shift with any degree of ease." Here, for the six to ten weeks of the voyage, the slaves lived like animals. Under the best conditions, the trip was intolerable. When epidemics of dysentery or smallpox swept the ships, the trip was beyond endurance.[12]

The pain and legacy of inhuman treatment from this long and cruel experience are still with us today. They are manifest in certain intercultural realities. "The pain of the present sometimes seems overwhelming, but the reasons for it are rooted in the past."[13]

Historical Consciousness

"Historical consciousness" is a way to question the world we have taken for granted. It means a thirst to know and learn the lessons of the past through the conditions and intellectual and normative traditions that guide (or fail to guide) our society today. Historical consciousness ought also to be pastoral care's subject. The practice of pastoral care, or the care of souls, is frequently organized by the immediate crisis or difficulty at hand. When informed by traditions of psychotherapy, pastoral caregivers strive to bring change in the inner world of the sufferer and a consequent adaptation to the world outside. Interventions are normally made to reduce stress, attain insight into the difficulty at hand, relieve or adjust the present suffering, and enable sufferers to move forward with their lives. This is an important emphasis.

But it may not be apparent how a historical event, such as the Middle Passage, can be relevant for the present. Indeed, there is a line of argument that would suggest that the past has very little to offer our present enlightened and technologically advanced society. It may be further argued that the "forgotten" past does not influence present-day transactions. Ours is a society that eschews the past and proceeds on a need to forget.

For example, on November 5, 1996, the voters of California passed a proposition (209) ending "affirmative action." By so doing Californians stated, in effect, that preferential treatment on the basis of race, sex, color, ethnicity, or national origin was no longer needed to correct the wrongs of the past that stem from our country's legacy of racism, slavery, and gender and class discrimination. True, this is a controversial and complex issue with tightly woven arguments on all sides. It is not my intent to engage the arguments, but to raise the question, What in our history would inform us that discrimination and oppression no longer threaten American democracy?

Is it the case that Americans appear to learn little from the lessons of history? Russell Jacoby thinks so. He argues that social amnesia appears to be an ingrained feature of modern Western society.[14]

> Within psychology new theories and therapies replace old ones at an accelerating rate. In a dynamic society, Freud is too old to be a fashion, too new to be a classic. The phenomenon of the newer replacing the new is not confined to psychology; it is true in all realms of thought. The new not

only surpasses the old, but also displaces and dislodges it.
The ability as well as the desire to remember atrophies.[15]

We soon forget or willfully repress the things we once knew. Social amnesia
rather than historical memory influences the way we live in the present.

Narrative Agency and Pentimento

The word *pentimento* comes from the world of art. *Pentimento* is
the phenomenon of an earlier painting showing through a layer or
layers of paint on a canvas.[16] I use the term *pentimento* metaphorically
to suggest that the past "bleeds through" after it has been forgotten,
willfully repressed, or covered over by the present. This suggests
that there is always a relationship between a present and its past—
whether recognized or not.

Historical consciousness is a vital resource for American pastoral
care. We must engage it if we are to better understand ourselves and
help shape a society worthy of human dwelling. The past has shaped
the present and lives on in the present in ways yet to be discovered.
By understanding the past, we internalize or incorporate it into our
everyday awareness and enable ourselves to use that understanding
to our advantage.[17] Internalization is the selective process of mapping
onto consciousness elements of experience that serve as a person's
intersubjective frame of reference. Internalization is one way the past
bleeds through events and relations and into our inner world. And
not everything that is internalized comes into awareness.

The past that bleeds through present day events and historical
memory can become a source that influences the way we understand
(or misunderstand) right relations with God, our ancestors, one
another, nature, and ourselves. Historical consciousness and
awareness of an historical event, such as the Middle Passage, can
also serve as a liberating agent rather than as mystification or a weight
that burdens and impedes forward movement. Historical
consciousness can enable us to comprehend what from the past is
bleeding through and how it is being absorbed in the present. Such
comprehension may help to form, reform, and transform
understandings of the present contexts in which we live, move, and
have our being. What, then, ought to be pastoral care's focus?

Historical consciousness further suggests that time is a whole—
past, present, and anticipated future. Therefore, it is deceptive to think
that we live only in the fleeting present. The past is always touching
the present. Hence, the meaning of lived experience is always complex

and ambiguous. The past represents ways of knowing that emerge from struggle and can inform us today. The complex and ambiguous present is the result of the experiences, thinking, and struggles of our ancestors who were born and raised in civilizations and circumstances different from our own. Their struggles birthed the conditions under which our consciousness develops and our life narrative unfolds. From them we may gain wisdom from patterns of living that extend an otherwise limited perspective on the present. John Lukas observes:

> For history the remembered past is not quite the same as history being memory. All living beings have a kind of unconscious memory; but the remembering of the past is something uniquely human, because it is conscious as well as unconscious, because it involves cognition together with recognition, because it involves thinking, and because human thinking always involves some kind of construction. I am interested in the evolution of this construction.[18]

This "construction" that evolves has roots in African, Asian, and European cultures, colonialism, and the conventions of White supremacy that helped to justify the traffic in Black cargo and that continues to be a conscious and unconscious feature of Western society—with damaging effects.

Damaging Effects of the Middle Passage

In the light of that historical event, the Middle Passage, there are certain invisible, transhistorical invariants that are still with us today. They are no longer associated with the sixteenth-century slave trade. I shall refer to certain transhistorical invariants as "damaging effects." They are among the invisible forces that move us.

I define damaging effects as the legacy of institutionalized practices and beliefs about Black inferiority and White superiority; inequities involving race, sexual orientation, gender, and class; and exploitive and oppressive conditions that still are determining human existence. They are those visible and invisible forces that destroy the bond between people and their communities, promote injustices, or aid physical, intellectual, emotional, and spiritual violence. In their turn interpersonal relationships, patterns, and trends can be carriers of damaging effects. People as well as systems themselves—the institutions and structures that weave society into an intricate fabric of power relations—can be carriers of damaging effects.[19]

A Perspective on Intercultural Realities

An example of damaging effects is seen in the inhuman treatment of Black slaves on the one hand, and the moral reasoning of the colonists that supported their vision for a new society on the other hand. The colonists, moving toward revolution, called for freedom and justice and pledged to seek liberty or death. The essence of their revolution was summoned up in the *Declaration of Independence*. It affirmed the equality of all people before God, the consent of the governed to be governed, and the inherent right to rebel against sustained oppression. And here were their enslaved Africans, who were denied freedom and put to death for rebelling. Damaged was the reflexive capacity to recognize contradiction and the many ways we deceive ourselves. Damaged was the moral foundation for freedom; damaged was a vision for a new society that respects cultural difference; damaged was an enlightened sense of democracy.

These damaging effects have been institutionalized and have a long history.[20] Social historian Ronald Takaki observes:

> In the English mind, the color Black was freighted with an array of negative images, "deeply stained with dirt," "foul," "dark or deadly" in purpose, "malignant," "sinister," "wicked." The color white, on the other hand, signified purity, innocence, and goodness.[21]

This symbolism also worked against certain ethnic groups, such as the Irish. Some came to America as White indentured servants. They shared a common social space of class exploitation with Blacks. According to Noel Ignatiev, "In the early years Irish were frequently referred to as 'niggers turned inside out.'"[22] But unlike Africans, they were not being conditioned for life-long servitude with the permanent status of property. Economic, cultural, social, and symbolic powers are among the transhistorical invariants that can be traced back to the slave trade. They underlie the motive force in social life that move us along—that is to say, "the pursuit of distinction, profit, power, wealth" and psychic, if not spiritual, well-being.[23]

The long history of institutionalized oppression includes the deliberate development of Jim Crow laws in all states from the end of the 1860s and the struggle against lynching. This long history was responded to by the development of Black schools and colleges from the last quarter of the nineteenth century. They were necessary to counteract the increasing exclusion of Black and other non-White children from good public education. *Brown* v. *Board of Education* capped a long struggle to develop a legal case against separate but equal schools.

Elizabeth Cady Stanton and Susan B. Anthony were nineteenth-century women who pioneered the women's rights movement in a time when they, like Black Americans, were excluded from full humanity. They knew the damaging effects of oppression and fought with women of color to transform it. Still, they were not completely free from the damaging effects of the Middle Passage. Racist and anti-immigrant forces were present in the movement. Their achievements have been largely forgotten. But present-day feminist writers who have built on their efforts continue to bring the awareness that gender, race, and class oppression are tied together. One such work is *Saved From Silence* by Mary Donovan Turner and Mary Lin Hudson.[24]

The struggle to transform damaging effects of the Middle Passage includes efforts by W. E. B. DuBois, people involved in the Harlem Renaissance, and other Black intellectuals in the early twentieth century.

Damaging effects of the Middle Passage are not limited to the past. They continue to bleed through after they have been forgotten and covered over by the present. The mid-twentieth-century civil rights movement took on the challenge of transforming the damaging effects of the Middle Passage. It built upon the steady but piecemeal gains of the 1940s and 1950s, the work of the NAACP, and the 1954 Supreme Court decision, *Brown v. Board of Education of Topeka, KS.* The civil rights movement officially began when a quiet but defiant Black woman, Rosa Parks, refused to give up her bus seat to a White passenger on December 1, 1955. It resulted in a successful bus boycott, the eventual dismantling of the Jim Crow laws in Southern states, the registration of Black voters in the Deep South, the Civil Rights Act of 1957—the first civil rights legislation to be passed since 1875— and the 1964 Civil Rights Law. *This long struggle against damaging effects of the Middle Passage unleashed forces of transformation that contributed to an ethos of resistance that made Rosa Parks's action thinkable.* This struggle, with some victories, did not happen without tragedy and great loss of life. The effects of the Middle Passage continued to bleed through! For example, we remember the bombing of the Sixteenth Street Baptist Church in Birmingham, where four Black girls were killed. Taylor Branch captures the scene with these words:

> On September 15 [the blast froze] the sanctuary clock at 10:22.
> A concussion of flying bricks and glass destroyed a bathroom

inside the staircase wall, where four adolescent girls were preparing to lead the annual Youth Day worship service at eleven, wearing white for the special occasion. Seconds later, a dazed man emerged clutching a dress shoe from the foot of his eleven-year-old granddaughter, one of four mangled corpses in the rubble. His sobbing hysteria spread around the world before nightfall. The Communist oracle *Izvestia* of Moscow raised a common cry with the Vatican newspaper in Rome, which bemoaned a "massacre of the innocents."[25]

The damaging effects of the Middle Passage were bleeding through! We remember the assassinations of Medgar Evers, Viola Liuzzo from Detroit, Rev. James Reebs, the three civil rights workers, Andrew Goodman, James Chaney, and Michael Schwerner. We remember the assassinations of Malcolm X and Martin Luther King Jr. And there were many more. As a result of the mid-twentieth-century civil rights struggle, some attitudes and stereotypes began to change, and African Americans began to be accepted in places where they had never been or were never allowed, such as in universities and seminaries as students, staff, or faculty.

The legacy of the Middle Passage's damaging effects continues to bleed through. Harvard sociologist William Julius Wilson gives us a glimpse of how the damaging effects of the Middle Passage continue to bleed through the social organization of everyday life in impoverished Black communities. Wilson does not use the term *damaging effects*. Instead, he uses the term *social dislocation* to describe the cycles of deprivation that have characterized urban ghetto neighborhoods since the mid 1960s. *Social dislocation* is a term that identifies significant changes in the social organization of inner-city communities, one of the most serious domestic problems in the United States today. Social dislocation may be characterized by low aspirations, poor education, family instability, illegitimacy, unemployment, crime, drug addiction and alcoholism, frequent illness, and Black-on-Black violence and early death.[26] In this way, Wilson identifies the lingering effects of the Middle Passage.

In recent years a general social survey was conducted by the National Opinion Research Center of the University of Chicago.[27] They have been doing public opinion research on matters of race since 1940. They were interested in gauging racial stereotypes of Blacks, Whites, Hispanics, and Asians. African Americans were compared with other racial groups in terms of work ethic, preference for welfare, and degree of intelligence. According to Wilson,

These relative judgments reveal that "Blacks are rated as less intelligent, more violence prone, lazier, less patriotic, and more likely to prefer living off welfare than whites." Not only are whites rated more favorably than Blacks, but on four of the five traits examined [with patriotism the exception]... many whites rated the majority of Blacks as possessing negative qualities and the majority of whites as possessing positive qualities.[28]

The damaging effects of the Middle Passage continue to bleed through!

The Middle Passage suggests important lessons for pastoral caregivers, ministers, and mental health workers. First, *anger*, and its more intense form, *rage*, and the hate rage begets, the kind that can only come from calculated cruelty and violation, needs to be acknowledged and appropriate channels of expression found. Black psychiatrists William Grier and Price Cobbs argue that White Americans do not want to hear it, and Black Americans are likely to turn it in upon themselves.[29] Anger, when distinguished from hate, can also be an indispensable force for change. It can be channeled toward analysis, protest, survival, and justice. Womanist theologian Cheryl A. Kirk-Duggan argues that "anger concerns justice because we can use anger to destroy self and others by choosing evil, or we can use anger to empower ourselves and others by choosing good. Anger as transformed energy can bring growth and healing—the use of anger for good."[30] Further, professionals, theologians, and health care practitioners must recognize that the damaging effects, which have their origin in objective historical and social conditions, are systemic and personal and need to be viewed developmentally as well as socially and historically. The sense of betrayal and loss of trust and freedom are profound, are rooted in collective memory, and give rise to a deep yearning for lasting freedom and self-determination. The experience of being devalued is acutely felt and gives rise to a search for a valued self, collective pride, and affirmation.

In sum, inhuman treatment is an undeniable feature of human experience. It is a paradigmatic part of Black experience in White society and can give rise to despair, hopelessness, and violence or to the quest for love, justice, and power in healing relationships.

It is not surprising, then, that we would place the damaging effects of the Middle Passage on the agenda of practitioners, pastoral care theologians, and the students who study with us. True, "damaging effects" come from other historical events, institutionalized practices, and unequal power relations and therefore cannot be viewed as coming only from the Middle Passage. The Middle Passage itself was part of a larger sequence of events that forever separated some Africans from their homeland. It is marked by the betrayal of Africans by Africans, their capture by White slavers, horrific conditions in the overcrowded barracks where the slaves were kept before their crossing of the Atlantic, horrific conditions on the slave ships, and their status as chattel slaves as they entered the New World. With a belief in a relational God and Divine Providence, pastoral care theologians may be challenged to make the connections between damaging effects of long-term historical trauma, such as the Middle Passage, and issues of internalized oppression, hopelessness, and rage; political impotence and lowered self-esteem; injustice; social dislocation; and structural oppression. Would not this be a legitimate focus for American pastoral care in the future?

Vignettes of Damaging Effects

In the following three vignettes we continue the claim that the pain of the present has roots in the legacy and damaging effects of the Middle Passage. If we can recognize the relevance of this claim, then it may serve as a context for identifying what can be distinctive about American pastoral care in the twenty-first century in general and African American pastoral care in particular. As we shall see, what is distinctive or typical about African American pastoral care is a belief in Divine Providence, a personal God who cares and is the ultimate relationship and ground of purpose, meaning, and hope, especially in the face of radical evil and suffering, injustice, and life-and-death problems. The person healing is one who works for justice and becomes a living witness to this Divine presence. From this perspective, God is ever moving toward us with a surging fullness...seeking to fill the little creeks and bays of our lives with unlimited resources.[31]

Vignette #1

Recently, Archie was asked by an attorney to write a declaration that might be part of a last-minute appeal to a state Supreme Court to stay the execution of an African American man, Manuel Pina Babbitt. The attorney was looking for someone with expertise on the effects of racism on African Americans and thought that perhaps Archie could help. According to news reports, the defendant's original court proceedings were marred by racial bias and judicial misconduct.

The original defense attorney was said to have used racial slurs when preparing for trial and did not want African Americans on the jury because "the average nigger" was "unreliable and could not understand a death penalty case."[32]

According to the May 3 edition of the *San Francisco Examiner*, the defendant requested that his attorney include Blacks and Hispanics in the jury pool. The news item continued: "The lawyer told him that those jurors were not of the caliber necessary to understand the evidence." His lawyer told Babbitt himself that he was "too ignorant and incoherent to take the stand and tell the jury [his] story." Later, "The lawyer consistently used derogatory racial terms, didn't trust Blacks and had three to four double vodkas or other drinks during lunch at the trial."[33]

David Kaczynski, the brother of Unabomber Theodore Kaczynski, "noted that his brother, who is white, pleaded guilty to three murders and got a bargained sentence of life without parole." Kaczynski "questioned whether Babbitt, who is Black, got impartial justice from the all white jury that sentenced him to death."[34] Paula Allen-Meares and Sondra Burman observed, "Because the justice system places a higher value on white men than on African American men, the latter have had disproportionately higher incarceration and death penalty rates. Investigations of crimes against African Americans are given low priority. Crimes against white people are more stringently punished."[35]

Granted, this was a complex case. The defendant was convicted of murder and spent years (1982–1999) on death row. The defendant never denied the charges. He did not doubt that he had committed the murder of a seventy-eight-year-old defenseless White woman, but he had no memory of it. I include this story because it illustrates the murderous rage and devaluation of personhood that is a part of the legacy and damaging effects of the Middle Passage. It destroys Black and White, and by extension everyone. It illustrates the cumulative and continuing significance of race for many African Americans who are disenfranchised and sometimes turn against themselves and others in a cycle of violent behavior and victimization.

According to news reports, the defendant suffered from mental illness as a child and suffered shell shock as a Marine at Khe Sanh in one of the bloodiest encounters of the Vietnam war, which lasted seventy-seven days. After the war he was diagnosed with paranoid schizophrenia, a typical diagnosis for African Americans suffering a mental disorder.[36] He also suffered post-traumatic stress as a Vietnam veteran, repeatedly ran into trouble with the law, became homeless, lost his wife and children, and spent time in prison and a mental hospital.[37]

The appeal for a new trial only delayed his execution for a half hour while the United States Supreme Court considered his final appeal. Babbitt had fasted for two days and forewent his last meal. He asked that it be given to a homeless person. He said to his attorney, "God has different ways of calling us home and this is the way he's chosen for me."[38] Manuel Pina Babbitt was executed on May 4 at 12:31 am. I did not know him personally. I only knew of his situation through the media. But I felt a profound sense of sadness when he was executed. The past bled through and played itself out in the present, and like so many others, his life was filled with frustration, pain, and trauma. Years of betrayal and loss of trust turned to despair and low self-esteem. These turned into anger and became forces of uncontrollable rage, destruction, and homicide. His life was devalued, and "the devaluation of African Americans and their culture can result in psychological scarring, violence and victimization."[39] In turn, he learned to devalue and destroy the lives of others. Rage gave birth to revenge and tragedy.

The governor was right to argue that difficult personal circumstances cannot justify the cruel beating and killing of a defenseless, law-abiding citizen. Nothing can justify such action. But was the governor justified in sanctioning the execution of Manuel Pina Babbitt—a life for a life? Did the Middle Passage affect the governor? I assume so, in as much as he is a product of American institutions and society. The dominant economic, political, social, and ideological forces that help determine life in American society have shaped him. Californians remember that in 1978 a White councilman, Dan White, assassinated San Francisco mayor George Mascone and councilman Harvey Milk. White was sentenced to four years in prison for his double murder. Journalist Jay Severin notes, "[T]he majority of convicted murderers are not executed even when their crimes are hideous, snuffing out the lives of children and innocent family members. Indeed, life sentences regularly feature relatively short prison terms, parole, release and, not infrequently, another murder."[40] Again, the Unabomber, who is White, was convicted of three murders and got life without parole, while Babbitt, who is Black, got the death penalty for one murder. Whether acknowledged or not, the governor's decision was consistent with a long tradition of discriminatory practices and oppressive conditions that have roots in the Middle Passage. Grier and Cobbs observed that a contempt and hatred of Black people is so thoroughly a part of the American personality that a profound convulsion of society may be required to help a dark child over his fear of the dark." Was the past bleeding through?

Vignette #2

The legacy and damaging effects of the Middle Passage can still be felt in certain institutionalized practices that affect the family life of African Americans. This legacy can be recognized in the words of Marian Wright Edelman: "A Black child still lacks a fair chance to live, learn, thrive, and contribute in America."[41] Edelman continues, "A Black child's father is 70 percent more likely than a white child's father to be unemployed, and when Black fathers find work, they bring home $70 a week less than white fathers. When both parents work, they earn only half what a white father earns."[42]

Recently, I was involved in helping a young African American father in his early twenties to gain the adoption of two children through the court. I shall refer to him as John. The ages of the children were two and five. The young mother of the children had suddenly taken ill and went into a coma. She died shortly after being rushed to the hospital. The deceased mother and the father were not married. John was the biological father of only one of the two boys. He wanted to adopt both of them because they had formed a bond, and he wanted to keep his family together. This young father also had been involved with trafficking in drugs and had been in trouble with the law. He was now trying to settle down, turn his life around, and become a responsible parent.

After the death of his partner, John moved one hundred and fifty miles to a different city. The family of his deceased partner wanted to take the children. But John did not want this, in part, because of their involvement with the drug culture that John was trying to leave behind. He moved, taking his two boys with him. He went to live with his mother, whom I shall call Martha. Martha is a very devoted and practicing religious woman. She made it clear that if the boys were to live with her, they had to observe certain religious principles such as prayer at meal times, church attendance, observation of the Sabbath, and treating one another with respect. She offered to help raise the boys and requested that John, her son, get a job and return to school. Both of these things he did.

The family of the deceased mother (which was also Black) did not want John to have custody of the boys and went to court to block his adoption. The White attorneys and caseworkers that supported the family of the deceased mother showed little regard for Martha's religious values. They told her that she was too religious. They asked if she could not miss going to church sometimes in order to accommodate the boys' weekly weekend scheduled visitation to their mother's family some hundred and fifty miles away. John and his mother Martha rely on public transportation, so traveling is always a challenge. Martha believed that the attorneys (including her own) and the caseworkers devalued her religious beliefs and worked to undermine her attempts to provide nurture and consistent moral and family values for the children who had come to live with her.

John, his two boys, and Martha entered into family therapy with me shortly after the death of the boys' mother. The goal was to establish a secure base in therapy so that the boys could express their feelings through play and the adults could talk about the recent loss of John's partner and how they might cooperate in establishing a new and nurturing home environment.

This was new territory for everyone. John L. McAdoo observes that the social science literature that explores the constructive role of the young Black father in the socialization of his children is almost nonexistent: "The Black father is usually seen as an invisible man who is not active in and has no power, control, or interest in the socialization of his children."[13] These goals for therapy were enhanced by the fact that Martha's religious values help to provide a moral framework and a safe and nurturing environment at home where the children are loved, clothed, and fed and have consistent adult supervision. When I began my work with John's family, the children were eager to participate in the therapy sessions. They were content, easily moved back and forth between the adults, and would play together, sometimes independently. But when the visitations began, there was an observed change in the behavior of the children and alarm on the part of the adults, John and his mother, Martha. The children were less eager to explore and appeared anxious and clingy. Martha reported that the younger child had night terrors and would wake up with loud cries. The older boy would wet his pants. Neither child had been doing these things before the visits began. The adults expressed concern about what the courts were doing and the disruptions that were created by the children being moved back and forth from one home to another.

Because of her own experience with family court over the years, Martha had come to believe that the secular court system does no value or even try to understand Black culture and works to destroy Black families under the guise of helping them. She felt that the new direction John was moving in and the stable home life she was trying to provide was being undermined. The effectiveness of the Black father in his role as a provider is viewed as dependent on his ability to aid in supporting his family and to share the provider role, thus legitimizing his authority within the family and allowing him to serve as a model of responsible behavior to his children.[44]

Martha expressed concern that if her son John were not successful in keeping his family, then he might experience this loss as failure, become discouraged and revengeful, and act it out in destructive ways.

Vignette #3

Jonestown and the mass suicide/murders are events that most have forgotten about. It began as an agricultural project established by a San Francisco–based church called the Peoples Temple. In the late 1970s they moved some of their operations to the remote jungles of northwest Guyana. Their goal was to establish an ideal religious community, a utopia. But on November 18, 1978, one of the most bizarre episodes in American religious history took place. On that day a U.S. Congressman and four others were assassinated at the Port Kaituma airstrip, followed by the mass suicide/murder of more than nine hundred people. More recent reports suggest 864 (September 1999). *Newsweek* referred to the Jonestown Commune as "a cult." The White press constructed them pejoratively as kooks, losers, dysfunctional, poor, and disturbed individuals who mindlessly followed a madman to their death. The folk who joined the Peoples Temple were from many walks of life and ranged widely in their motives, lifestyles, and values orientations. More than 70 percent were Black; 23 percent were White; and 6 percent were Native American, Latino, Asian, and Mexican American. Many were women, children, and senior citizens.[45] They were young and old, from wealthy as well as poor backgrounds, well-educated and illiterate, widowed and married, single parents as well as husbands and wives, the religiously committed as well as those who were indifferent to religion.[46] Barbara ⁓ ʰⁿ Moore lost two daughters and a grandchild at Jonestown. ⁓ said that the followers were incredibly idealistic and ⁓. She reminded us that the Peoples Temple had been ⁓ing the Kennedy/Vietnam era of concern for people of every race and condition. The members of Peoples Temple were committed to caring for all kinds of people.[47]

No one knows the full truth of what exactly happened. But one may surmise that even in this utopian commune, the members' vision was not broad or critical enough to perceive the barriers of class, sex, age, and race within the social structure of the organization itself. The past bled through. The top echelon and key decision-makers were White, educated professionals calling the shots that determined and sealed the fate of the significantly Black membership, mostly women, many elderly, who had given up everything to follow Jones. According to Jeannie Mills's account, "There were attorneys, college professors, a man who had graduated with honors from MIT, social workers, nurses, businessmen, and lots of other professional people on that council."[48]

Whether intended or not, the movement itself perpetuated an established relational pattern of superior-inferior power relationships in the Peoples Temple. It was a pattern that has been characteristic of race relations in the West since the sixteenth and seventeenth centuries. The leadership was primarily White and educated, with a few token Blacks. The followers were the masses of predominantly Black and minority group members. The vulnerable position of Blacks and women in the Peoples Temple reflected their position of vulnerability in the wider society. The ruling elite and their power to shape the social outlook functioned to perpetuate inequality within the group and to control the flow of communication. The past was bleeding through. The belief in freedom and equality that some assumed was there was a false consciousness. This belief misrepresented the true subordinate position of Blacks within the group. Had there been the freedom and opportunity to engage systemic thinking by reflecting on and critically analyze their situation, then critical questioning of the social process and an opportunity to radically change it may have been possible. The damaging effects of the Middle Passage bled through and found expression in the people themselves. They were the real victims of a system, which they supported or rationalized and were powerless to change. The tragedy, known as "Jonestown," had deep roots in the conventions of White supremacy.

The legacy of the Middle Passage points to the continuing and subtle effects of institutionalized racism as a form of unilateral power, resulting in subordinate social positions, frustration, hopelessness, and uncontrollable rage, which in their turn become forces of destruction—violence, homicide, suicide. We saw evidence of this in the case of Manuel P. Babbitt and in the Peoples Temple movement. How can such vicious cycles be broken and then transformed?

In his book *The Color of Faith* theologian Fumitaka Matsuoka observes that it is hard to trust those who do not share your history of common struggle and who are the heirs of those who have inflicted historical injuries.[49] What we need, he argues, is a way of relating to one another about mutual relatability, intelligibility, and interdependence that goes beyond binary, adversarial, and appositional discourse of human relations. What we are faced with today are attempts to redescribe the other so that they "fit the image and expectations of the dominant culture. Only then, can members of the dominant culture be 'sensitive' to questions of cruelty and humiliation."[50] When the world is redescribed in terms of one's subjectivity, those who are different can have no real existence. Silence deepens, or a romanticized notion of unity exists. An unwillingness to deal with historical outsiders and the radically different is never recognized. There is today a new silence, neglect, misunderstanding, and concealment about matters of race and class. Such silence and neglect limits us to conversations with like-minded people. Such a posture not only promotes historical injuries but also hinders the search for a better America and a better world.[51] The failure of communication leads to an erosion of relationships and to an increased inability to acknowledge historically developed patterns of violence.[52] There is a strong tendency to adapt a posture of color and class blindness. In reality, this posture perpetuates dominant positions of power and injustice. Such a posture does not allow one to see. Rather, it contributes to not seeing, ignorance, further silence, and lack of communication on issues that really make a difference. "In such a world there is not genuine relationship, but opposition, suspicion, and distrust."[53]

The three vignettes above suggest that the law, religion, education, and the family are among the contexts for pastoral care interventions, especially for African American pastoral care.

III

Systemic Awareness

Any view of pastoral care that would derive from the Middle Passage would recognize that none of us could escape or live outside of the power and patterns of history. Human existence is historical existence. And where we stand today, whether recognized or not, has its origin in the past.

People often have the sense of being moved by obscure forces within themselves, which they are unable to define or explain. And without a historical consciousness, they may not be able to imagine how such forces may work toward the end of human betterment. As educators and pastoral care providers and systemic thinkers, it would be central to our task to develop a quality of mind that seeks to understand the intimate realities of us in connection with larger social forces.

If it is true that each of us lives out a narrative within some historical sequence and contributes, however minutely, to the shaping of society and the course of history, then it is important to have an imagination that is able to make connections between history and biography within society and culture.

Ideally, a sense of caring arises and structures of justice multiply when love, trust, and forgiveness are repeated experiences in community. Frequently, a sense of gratitude is a by-product of being in a caring relationship. Truly grateful people tend to share their joy, and such experiences can help counter the damaging effects of oppression, loneliness, despair, and hopelessness.

One cannot speak about Christian African American pastoral care without speaking about Black communities, the Black church, and other Black religious institutions. The Black church and other Black religious institutions are a part of the culture that is caught in cycles of violence and mediates the damaging effects of oppression. Black religious institutions are also responsive to transcendent norms such as justice, agape, and faithfulness. Hence, the Black church is both in the world as agent of hope and of the world as carrier of its values and norms. Ideally, it aims to organize its life according to relational principles—transcendent values, gospel, and theological norms that can help discern God's purposes for human dwelling and human transformation amidst the damaging effects of oppression. This should be the subject of Christian African American pastoral care.

Divine activity, not only the training of the therapist, is recognized as the primary healing agent in African American pastoral care. God calls on a people in bondage, reaches through suffering, touches their pain, frees them from oppression, inspires hope, and continues to work with them to transform radical evil.

Therefore, my perspective on pastoral care in America is shaped by my experience as an African American male and a member of the community. African American pastoral care's emphasis is systemic and relational in its approach. It values narrative agency and is sensitive to the difference that culture makes. This requires us to think in terms of social power arrangements and their invisible, unrecognized effects. It requires us to observe interactions and notice sequence, patterns, and context. We must understand the ways in which meaning is being constructed, as we saw in the cases of Manual Babbitt, John and Martha, and Jonestown. African American pastoral care remains vigilant to how the past bleeds through into the present. It is a perspective and practice that is informed by a historical consciousness and leads us to think about how events, behavior, and emotion—the small details of story—are woven together and become part of a wider and unfolding narrative.

Underlying African American pastoral care is a daring belief that people can be changed and can work to resist, if not transform, the damaging effects of systemic evil.

Conclusion

The damaging effects of the Middle Passage bleed through in the continued exploitation and oppression of African Americans. All Americans are affected in some way. Our task as teachers, preachers, practitioners, and scholars is to help develop the capacity for historical consciousness and to engage systemic thinking by making the connections between our historic past and the ever-emerging present. Our aim is a more just and compassionate world. Marian Wright Edelman reflected on those who mentored her toward a more just and compassionate world. She wrote:

> Who knows what emboldened Mrs. [Rosa] Parks in 1955 not to move after riding segregated buses all her life? Was it her tired feet or her tired soul saying enough, or the seeds from the Highlander Folk School citizenship training she had attended some weeks before, or all of these? Perhaps sharing time and grievance with others from across the South and feeling part of a community of fellow strugglers unleashed long repressed emotions and courage.[54]

As students, ministers, teachers, supervisors, and practitioners of pastoral care, we are mentors. We are witness to an ever-emerging power that works in and among us to transform damaging effects. In the words of the apostle Paul, "We have this treasure in clay jars, so that it may be made clear that this extraordinary power belongs to

God and does not come from us."[55] This means that pastoral caregivers are witnesses. A witness is not a passive observer with a silent voice, but a participant who works in hope and as a co-creator actively shaping (and being shaped by) his or her emerging diverse and rich environment. This means that one must ultimately trust in God, that God works through human efforts to bring good out of cruel and collective suffering. This belief in divine redemption is the foundation for a moral vision. We cannot guarantee the good through our own efforts alone. Good and evil live in constant struggle, whether hidden in ambiguity or revealed in stark clarity.[56] Whatever we do as individuals, as family members, or as a group is never, in itself, sufficient to guarantee the good indefinitely. What we can do is become aware of the history that has shaped us. Aware of our historical past, and with a sense of narrative agency, we can self-consciously work for the good, confess our limitations, stay alert to every new and emerging form of evil, and challenge our students, colleagues, family members, individuals, and groups to develop their own practices and traditions of care, prayer, and work for spiritual discernment. Evil and suffering may not always be thwarted in the forces of history, but the hopes and struggles for progress toward the goals of redemption in individual, family, and social life; the values of love, justice, and peace; and the common good are effective when operative in human life.[57] The norms of love, power, and justice can go a long way in countering the damaging effects of oppression and helping people to live creatively amidst suffering in their present life and to conjure hope for the future. Paul Tillich helped us to see that love, power, and justice are dynamic principles in moral life and that they are interrelated in the divine reality. They are the basis for the experience of genuine sorrow, which implies not only the desire for future amendment of life but also the desire to repair or minimize the injuries inflicted on others. When power is abused, justice is thwarted and love fails to be realized. Love, power, and justice can serve as norms for countering the damaging effects of oppression and enhance human or narrative agency that has its source in the being and agency of God. Such forces can counter the damaging effects of oppression.

American Church historian Eldon Gilbert Ernst observed:

> If it is true that love in practice is the greater power in personal life as well as in social environments, and that supreme love ultimately reigns victorious over the persistence of hate,

injustice, greed, and violence with each new generation, then perhaps we can experience a kind of existential hope within the dialectic of historical realism and eschatological idealism. If so, then not in vain will the values of love, justice, peace and the common good direct our lives here and now. We, too, are part of history. Life can be better rather than worse at any time and place, and even we can unleash forces that help to overcome evil in the world. Still, valleys as well as mountain tops will remain in our lives and in history past, present, and future.[58]

Pastoral care in America that is informed by a historical consciousness and the Middle Passage can lead to this kind of prodigious hope. It can help form tributaries that join with other streams or traditions of pastoral care, which in their confluence give inspiration and a kind of fluid and surpassing hope that might otherwise elude us.

EXERCISE

In this chapter we showed there are connections to be made between a past and a present, between a historical event and contemporary pastoral care. Contemporary pastoral care emerges from ongoing historical processes. It carries a legacy that is covered over by more current thinking and practices, which emerge from immediate responses to the vicissitudes of life. Different understandings of the past shape our context and influence our responses to the issues at hand, whether acknowledged or not. The concept *pentimento* was borrowed from the world of art. An artist may take a canvas and paint a picture, but over time the canvas may be used many times, and layer upon layer of different colors of paint will be applied. The original paint will be buried ever deeper with each new layer. But eventually, the top layer wears off with age, and the earlier paintings, a profusion of colors and/or images, begin to bleed though. Hence, the past touches the present in surprising and sometimes disturbing ways. We used this idea of *pentimento* as metaphor for interpreting what is going on in personal, social, and political life.

1. Write a memory from your own personal life or from the life of someone close to you. Identify "something" that happened that over time was forgotten about and buried beneath other experiences. A recent event may trigger memory of the earlier event. It begins to bleed through. Write about how the "bleeding through" occurred and with what consequences for narrative agency.

2. Select a historical event to write about. It could be a perspective on wars or a social or political movement (forceful removal of Native Americans, 1838; Trail of Tears; Women's Rights Convention at Seneca Falls, 1848; WWII and Pearl Harbor, 1941; twentieth-century Jewish Holocaust in Nazi Germany; atom bomb dropped on Hiroshima and Nagasaki by the United States; U.S. Supreme Court decision *Brown* v. *Board of Education*, 1954; Vietnam War, 1950–60s); a scientific breakthrough, such as "the Pill," 1960; a religious event, such as the Reformation, Great Awakening, or an epoch change such as the Enlightenment following the Middle Ages; a perspective on a catastrophe such as the bubonic plague (1330–1600s) or the Great Potato Famine

(1845–1850). These are examples of a historical event. You may wish to select a perspective on a historical event of your own choosing. Reflect on how influences from the past that you selected continues to bleed through into our (postmodern) times and with what effects. How can we derive from history any illumination of our present condition? How can we derive guidance for our judgments and practices about doing God's will? How do we become siblings by choice?

6

Gender Change and Cultural Traditions

Pastoral care's excessive preoccupation with emotion, feeling, and "heart" led to a countermovement...to recover wholeness for pastoral care. Its focus is the cognitive orientation of pastoral care. How we feel (cathectic orientation) depends significantly on our reality assumptions (cognitive orientations). What we decide is right and ethical (evaluative orientation) hinges also on our epistemology (the cognitive). Pastoral care has bought heavily into the cultural pluralism and cognitive relativism of modern culture: as caregivers, we see our role as supporting people along the road they have chosen, of being agenda-free, and of being client—(or person) centered. Norms of tolerance and acceptance of others' viewpoints so dominate present-day pastoral care that care-givers are left confused and ambivalent about their identity as religious counselors and about the value of their theological tradition in the counseling process.

George Furniss[1]

I

Pastoral care providers are frequently presented with problems that appear to repeat themselves. Some problems, such as violent or abusive behavior, may appear to be resistant to change. "People who have endured horrible events," for example, "suffer predictable psychological harm."[2] According to research psychiatrist Judith

Herman, "There is a spectrum of traumatic disorders, ranging from the effects of a single overwhelming event to the more complicated effects of prolonged and repeated abuse. Established diagnostic concepts, especially the severe personality disorders commonly diagnosed in women, have generally failed to recognize the impact of victimization."[3] Can a similar statement be made about men? In the movie *Chocolat,* a priest counseled with an abusive parishioner after his wife left him. After a period of time the husband declared himself "changed." He wanted to reconcile with his wife. But when she refused his gesture of reconciliation, he became violent again. How do pastoral care providers decide when someone has changed or not? Does change come from insight or only from within? Or are other forces operating? In short, how do pastoral care providers account for human change?

How do people change? People rarely change because you tell them to. How do you get people to change their habits, minds, beliefs, values, attitudes, or behavior, such as practicing discrimination, developing drinking or smoking addictions, participating in abuse, and so forth. Do the changes we think we make last? How or why do we sometimes relapse? The question "How do people change" is often perplexing for change agents such as parents, educators, psychologists and social scientists, law-enforcement personnel, social reformers, partners, ministers, and therapists.

Perhaps a more intriguing question is, "Why do people appear not to change?" If change is all around us and in us, and if we are always in flux, then why do people, and some things, appear not to change, particularly when they desire it? There is a commonly voiced view in the therapy world that *only you can change yourself,* no one else can change you, or that change only comes from insight or from within. If this is the case, then we are the directors of our own destiny. Are we? People have free choice, or do they? If we are in control and can will our own change, then why is it that some of the things we will do not appear to change? How do women and men change or seem to remain the same in relationship to self and/or cultural traditions? Perhaps human change is more complex than we normally think. There are material and invisible forces that operate from within and from without—principalities and powers—that may influence the changes we think we are making. We cannot be aware of them all. Can we predict the future based on our observations of the past (and, we might ask, which past and whose future)? Can we control the direction and magnitude of change? We still know very little about how to "guard against the rebuffs of surprise or the vicissitudes of change."[4] We explore these questions. We want to show some complexities of human change and to bracket a naive assumption that we, individually, are in charge of our own change and that change only comes from willing it, from insight, or from within.

II

What do counselors, supervisors, and professors of pastoral care need to know about human change and cultural traditions of the women and men with whom they work in order to understand the situations they are in? If it is the case that we live within layer upon layer of story, then perhaps we can learn about the vicissitude of human change when we turn to history and cultural traditions for illumination or guidance. First, we will situate this discussion of change by acknowledging the contributions of biologists who have influenced the field of psychotherapy. Their assessments have implications for pastoral care because of their views of living systems and change. Second, we shall discuss change and cultural traditions in the context of "stories of origin."

III

A Biological Perspective on Change

Biologists and Chilenian scholars Humberto Maturana and Francisco Varela[5] argue that all living systems (biological structures) are self-determining; they have an environment and an active relationship with other living systems that are purposeful, goal-seeking, and self-organizing. The goal-seeking and self-organizing activities of biological structures or living systems account for certain change. Living human systems are responsive—that is, they give and receive influences. Living beings are thinking, feeling, deliberating, negotiating, and adapting to their environment, which itself is changing in response to human activity. We adapt to war, famine, and natural disasters, for example. We adapt to changing weather patterns by seeking ways to keep warm, especially in the cold of winter. We may accumulate more than we can use or create artificial fuel, which may pollute the air. We dump waste or toxic chemicals into the ground or water, pollute our streams, and diminish freshwater supplies. When we engage in such activities, we change, and our environment changes also. New life forms may appear, and old ones may die. We must learn to positively adapt to the changes in the ecological system if we wish to survive. We must care as if our very lives depended on it. The environment, the living ecological system of which we are part, responds to our activities over time. In this way, living systems are responsive, adapting, creating, and, therefore, always changing. Living systems change their structures when environmental conditions change. In this process of change, living systems achieve a higher level of complexity, thereby improving their chances for continued survival. Those living systems that become extinct may have become so because of natural catastrophe, changes in the ecological system, or the inability to adapt to an environment that could no longer support their life form. The human living system is influenced by its own structure, reproductive capacity, environmental conditions, context, and cultural patterns; by resources developed over time; and by repeating successful experiences.

According to Maturana and Varela, living beings are structurally determined systems; that is to say, they operate according to the way they are made. The central nervous system plays an important role in adaptation and survival. It is a closed system of neurons within the living organism that enables successful interactions with the environment. It exists in dynamic interdependence with the environment. Key to survival or successful interaction between organism and environment is the flow of information that helps to bring about beneficial adaptations, but the adaptations are determined by the *structure* of the organism. Hence, how living humans perceive and organize themselves around the flow of information between themselves and the environment depends on its structure, and the interplay between structure and environment is crucial to their survival.

Maturana and Varela state that perception is produced in the brain. The brain develops its own language and ways of knowing. "Recall" or "remembering" plays an important role in the way the brain organizes information according to hierarchies. Memories help the brain to create a connection between the inside and outside worlds. Consciousness, according to their theory, is not located within the brain; rather, it is a product of the organism as a whole. It is a roadmap that guides the living organism through the environment. Consciousness is the interaction between the central nervous system and its environment. Consciousness, then, is related to the "ego" and "self." The ego develops in the context of early human relationships and develops a particular structure, style, or characteristic way of processing and remembering information about self in the world.

The ego is a complex construction. It organizes experience that includes its structure and perception of the body, relationships, and the interplay between thoughts and feelings.

Living human systems, following Maturana and Varela, are "autopoietic"—self-organizing—producing and stabilizing their organization by ongoing interaction within the body and with others. Together, living human organisms create networks that produce and reproduce themselves in terms of similarity and difference. In order to maintain balance, living systems tend to expect things to happen according to plans that are based on past experience. In this way, adaptation to the environment and a sense of sameness or familiarity appears assured. At the same time, unexpected and unplanned or different and unfamiliar things happen, and new responses are required of the living organism. According to this theory, change occurs through mechanisms and processes of adaptation and reorganization in relationship to environmental change. These changes are not willed; rather, they are a part of natural or biological processes. Maturana and Varela give us a biological basis for thinking about human change and suggest that change represents a complex relationship between living organisms and their internal and external environments. Such change is not always conscious, willful, or a result of insight. How pastoral care providers account for human change will depend, in part, on what role living human systems as biological structures play in their explanation of change. There is another level of explanation that we consider next.

A Culture Tradition Perspective

We turn to an ancient myth about violence and gender relations in order to appreciate the role of myth and cultural tradition in the assessment of why things appear to change or remain the same. Special attention is given to the story of Theseus and Ariadne, as told in ancient Greek mythology. By considering myth, we may come to see that change is not solely a matter of biological structures, emotions, or cognition, as important as these are. Change and resistance to change have cultural roots as well as biological, emotional, and cognitive ones. We use the Theseus and Ariadne myth to introduce the idea that stability and change have cultural roots. This myth is taken as a starting point for an "archeology of knowledge" (Foucault). Our point is that gender and violence have their roots in many different layers, some of which cultural. Cultural traditions underlay ideas about change and fur help us to appreciate why change is complex, difficult to achiev hard to sustain.

Layer #1: Theseus and the Labyrinth

A story in Greek mythology starts with the threat to Athens by King Minos from Crete.[6] Every year, Athens has to pay tribute to Minos by sending seven boys and seven girls to Crete to enter a bewildering maze, the labyrinth. When the yearly season came, the Crete King's son, Theseus, asked for the reason of the demand. He is told that king Minos had laid siege to Athens when it was but a small town. He would have let all the people starve to death if they had not agreed to sacrifice the lives of fourteen young men and women as payment each year. What a terrible price the Athenians agreed to pay. Every year, at the spring equinox, the people of Athens have to undergo a ritual of humiliation. They must send fourteen of their most promising youths to King Minos. The King then feeds them alive to a terrible monster called Minotaur, a beast—half bull and half human—kept inside the labyrinth because of his atrocious nature. The labyrinth, which was built by the famous Daedalus, has so many winding and bewildering paths that no one who enters it can ever find his or her way out again. Theseus, struck by his father's and the Atheneans' sorrow, decides to join the youths to be sent. He plans to kill the monster in order to free his country from this oppression. He takes two sails with him: a white one in case he returns as a victor, a black one in order to demonstrate defeat and mourning. When the ship reaches Crete, the young people are led into the king's presence. Theseus asks to be sent into the labyrinth by him. Ariadne, the beautiful daughter of King Minos, watches Theseus and falls in love with him. During the night, she provides him with a sword to kill the Minotaur and a ball of string to help him find his way out of the labyrinth. Theseus is to tie one end of the ball of thread to the entrance of the labyrinth and unravel the ball as he makes his way. In exchange, he promises to marry Ariadne and take her back to Athens. Theseus enters the labyrinth and, with help of the sword, slays the monster. He follows the string and finds his way out of the labyrinth. He takes Ariadne and his companions to his ship, burns the Cretan ships, and sails to Naxos, where he and Ariadne make love. While Ariadne is still sleeping, though, he leaves her behind in order to return to Athens. Ariadne is desperate when she wakes up. Theseus, coming close to Athens, forgets to exchange the black sail for the white one. His father sees the black sail from afar. Aegeus, the king of Athens, thinks that his son has perished and throws himself from a rock. He is killed. Theseus becomes the new king of Athens.

In the tradition of this story we find several versions of the ending, and none of them is a "happy" one. One version tells that Theseus leaves Ariadne alone on the island of Naxos, where she gives birth to two sons. Another version holds that Ariadne falls into despair when she realizes that Theseus has abandoned her. She commits suicide by hanging herself from a tree.

The Main Plot

Is this plot mere mirror of the ever-recurring themes and archetypes of human lives that are stored in collective memory and reexperienced in dreams and works of art regardless of difference in cultural backgrounds? If so, then the journey through the labyrinth would be typical for male development. The slaying of the Minotaur and the love and separation story of Theseus and Ariadne would be typical of male-female relations. Men are meant to strive for adventure, fight evil, and prize freedom over bonding. In this scenario, women are typically engulfed in relationships and assigned the roles of helpmate and caretakers of others—including children. Eventually, they are left to fend for themselves with longings for intimate connection. This view has been prevalent for centuries and revived in new theories. Is this the progression of change in gender relations that we are fated to live out? Are we culturally determined? These changes may not be solely a matter of will or a result of insight or structural determinism. There are unacknowledged cultural forces that also operate and can make difficult the kinds of changes we would like for our communities and ourselves. As we shall see, there are layers and layers of history and cultural forces at work that can impede and jeopardize the kind of change we desire. They may separate us and keep us from being siblings by choice. We refer to the concept *pentimento* from the world of art to suggest how we relate to the past. An artist may use a canvas to paint a picture. Over time, the original image is buried deeper and deeper and covered over by ever-new layers of paint. When the newest layer of paint begins to wear thin, then the underlying images that have been buried begin to bleed through into the present. *Pentimento* is a metaphor for our present relationship to the past. When the past is forgotten and covered over by newer interpretations of the self and for the workings of society, then unresolved and past traumatic experiences begin to bleed through. When present-day beliefs, images, and practices are unexamined, enshrined as sacred, and unquestioned, then they become resistant to new information or threatened by older interpretations of what is going on. The forgotten past has consequences for present-day realities and helps influence the direction of change.

The main plot is replicated in other myths and fairytales. For example, princess Medea helps Jason, an adversary hero, to gain a treasure precious to her kingdom. She leaves her home country behind. Common mythic themes that appear in the Medea story are the love of the princess for the young man, her help offered him to overcome obstacles, their flight together and the betrayal of her family of origin, her complicity in the murder of her own brother, and her abandonment by the hero after achieving his goal. These are familiar themes about gender relations in traditional fairytales. Many love songs of European background mirror the same narrative progression: The hero fights and overthrows evil, which is in the form of a beast or an enemy. The hero establishes his power on the death of another. The help of a female companion and her knowledge and love is central to the process of liberation, but not essential for the final establishment of his reign. The main interest engaging the reader is the power of fathers and their adversaries, followed by the reign of their heirs, their sons. Threat and use of violence, coercion, deception, and betrayal play an important role in all the mythology we know from the Greek and other Indo-European traditions.[7]

IV

The Labyrinth as Symbol and Influence

The labyrinth, as symbol, has attracted new attention in European and North American literature. The labyrinth, as maze, is a structure consisting of so many winding and bewildering paths that it is nearly impossible to find a way out. In European architecture there have been many famous constructions of mazes in parks and gardens. The maze has become a place for people to challenge their mind and courage as they move through winding corridors or encounter dead ends. The labyrinth, as metaphor, represents people getting lost in mazes of thought, memories, relationships, and political struggles. The Minotaur inside the maze has become a symbol for the evildoer or monster; the unfamiliar or strange; the deviants within our midst; the threat of gays, lesbians, questioning[8], or transgendered persons; those of mixed race; the condemned and undeserving poor. Fighting the monster and killing it is a preoccupation in Western tradition. The ones who fight and extinguish the "terrorists," the "axis of evil," the "evil empires," the "adversary" (whereever they are) are celebrated as "heroes," be it in sports; business; police or military combat; movies, games, or songs; or religious rituals. The Minotaur—the other, the stranger, the foreigner, the bad, the mad, the unknown, and so forth—is portrayed as the opposite, the source of irrationality and impurity, the enemy, and, therefore, the threat that has to be conquered and destroyed. Theseus, who has mastered the maze, is the winner. Once Theseus is king of Athens, it does not matter any more what happens to Ariadne or their offspring.

Yet the very identification of a maze and a labyrinth as erroneous, confusing, or bewildering demonstrates a loss of knowledge and memory within the dominant culture. There is another layer to be uncovered. Originally the labyrinth was not a building containing erroneous ways, but a symbol of a path. This path is not erroneous, but one of many leading toward a center. There, in the center, one has to turn around, and the same path returns to the entrance in a winding, meandering journey. Originally, it was not possible to lose oneself in a labyrinth. One only becomes stuck if one does not move forward or backward. If this version or layer has been ignored, then it may represent resistance to change or a loss of cultural knowledge.

The feeling of insecurity is connected to movement: One cannot foresee where the journey will end. Similarly, one cannot foresee and fully control the path of one's life. Drawings of labyrinths have been found on ancient seals and coins; on rocks; on the floors of palaces in the Mediterranean, Knossos, Israel, Greece, and Rome; and in cathedrals in France. Some labyrinths have been constructed by stones on a ground or mown into lawns (in Sweden and England) or on sand paintings and rocks (in Native Indian territories in North and South America). The labyrinth has been interpreted as a symbol of the way of life itself, leading a person back and forth and meandering through different phases of his or her life, during which he or she encounters crises and challenges. These challenges might be important life stages, such as encountering a partner, connecting in love and sexuality, giving birth, or experiencing illness and death. They may symbolize important crises in feeling, thinking, and acting, a transformation of mind, spirit, and soul. Or the labyrinth may represent the complex and confusing power struggles that often surface in social change movements, organizations, or liberation struggles.

Layer #2: Ariadne and the Labyrinth

There is another version of the Theseus and Ariadne story that may lead to a deeper meaning of the tradition. Ariadne is often connected to the labyrinth. Daedalus, the famous artist, created the labyrinth as a place for dance in which Ariadne and her maiden consorts performed ritual dances. Ancient traditions of ritual dance still exist in the Greek islands and France. The ancient dance consists of a chain of dancers moving back and forth, thus portraying the movement of the stars and the planets, which played an important role in the orientation and interpretation of the world and the universe in ancient times. This version of the myth opens up a different window, an older layer buried and covered over by a more recent layer of the story. In this older tradition, Ariadne is not the little princess who falls in love and is abandoned. Rather, she is a representation of the Great Goddess who reigned the universe, giving birth and recreating life from threats of crisis and death.

In all versions of the myth, Ariadne owns the golden ball of string. It is her ball of string that guides the human hero through the challenges of life. It is her sword that empowers and makes the difference between victory and defeat, life and death. Her knowledge and holding makes it possible to walk the path and face challenge and potential death with courage. She makes it possible for the hero to return to life in a new way, similar to the way nature returns to new life each year. The ball of string could be interpreted as the thread of life that connects us with the source of all life and guides humans through the sometimes confusing and bewildering phases of existence.

This second layer of the myth is supported by the research of the German scholar Hermann Kern, a leading expert in labyrinth research. According to Kern, the maze, constructed late in the Hellenistic period, was depicted as an architectural drawing on the floor, but was not a building. Both the maze and the labyrinth were the place of dance. Young women and men, leading toward a center, performed the dance winding back and forth. The rope (Ariadne's string) connects the dancers. They stay connected while moving in complex turns to the center. Sometimes the chorus lines moved counterclockwise, and sometimes clockwise. In the center, the first dancer was trapped (facing crisis) and could only move out if the line of dancers moved back or if they all turned around and faced in a new direction (adopting a new perspective or new worldview). In this tradition, the dance was part of initiation rituals. It offered opportunities to learn "the way of life," passing through phases of love, crisis, dangerous challenges, and back to new experiences of growth.

The belief that divine power and wisdom led the dancers guided this ritual experience. The one goddess—called Gaia, Rhea, Pasiphae,

Demeter, Artemis, or Ariadne—was the source of all life and death. Thus, the labyrinth dance symbolized the journey of life and death, a theme important to all mystery traditions in ancient spirituality. In this layer of the myth, Theseus represents human beings facing dangerous situations while growing up and maturing to understand more of the mystery of life, death, and rebirth.[9]

In another ending of the myth, the gods' will forces Theseus to leave Ariadne. Ariadne marries Dionysus, the god representing youth, growth, and ecstasy. The myth's combination of love, fertility, death, and new life refers to the spiritual tradition of matriarchal societies, which flourished especially in the Pre-Minoan time of Crete and other Mediterranean regions before the onset of classical Greek history. Developed matriarchal societies celebrated the sacred marriage each year as a symbolic interconnecting of divine and human, of universe and earthbound life, of female and male, of diverse energies uniting, mingling, and creating new life. Bull and cow were important symbols of fruitfulness that might explain the story of Ariadne's mother, Pasiphaë (another goddess), celebrating love as a cow with the bull, thus procreating the Minotaur.

Following Heide Goettner-Abendroth's interpretation, Ariadne is the moon-goddess, the light and the likeness of Demeter, the ancient mother goddess. Her consort was Dionysus, the child god of Crete, represented in the priest-king. His male fertility was symbolized in Aries, in the bull or the male goat, wearing the horns. Once a year, he symbolically died in the double axe of the goddess, the labrys, which were her symbols of the phases of the moon.[10] According to Barbara Walker, Ariadne was called "Most Holy," or "high fruitful mother," worshiped as a consort of Dionysus. Hellenic myth disparaged her and made her a mortal maiden.[11] Witness to the celebration of loving ecstasy and sacred marriage is still present in some of the wisdom traditions in biblical texts, such as the Song of Songs. The lovers sing of each other's beauty, longing and coming together in spite of all attempts to prevent them from loving.

Myths of origin make the roots of violence in gender relations visible. The classical Greek myth of Theseus who slays the monster can be seen as a prototype of European history. Conquest and destruction of highly developed ancient societies, cultures, and religions became a characteristic sign of "development." Deconstruction of the Theseus myth leads to the excavation of subjugated knowledge in narratives that give expression to more complex and respectful relations between women and men, humans and nature, and humans and the divine. In the deeper layers of the Ariadne myth we learn that women are honored as sources of life. Women and men, sisters and brothers are important as sustainers of life. The bond between humans, nature, and the divine are recognized as foundational for survival and creativity.

The labyrinth symbolizes life as process. The way of life is depicted as meandering, moving toward a turning point and back again toward a center. This circuitous process is never linear. It cannot be controlled. It always calls for motion, for openness to challenge and to transformation.

Remembering the labyrinth may help pastoral care providers and trainers account for destructive patterns in gender relations. Enlarged cultural narratives can empower transformation in relations between women and men of diverse cultural roots.

Our journey through this chapter encourages us to look at different layers of the cultural myths that underlie our perceptions and thinking about change. How do we describe and interpret the realities before us? Have we assumed much but learned little about the nature of change? Change occurs on many different levels and all the time, but how does it come about? We are still informed by the insight of Heraclitus: "You cannot step twice into the same river, for other waters are forever flowing." We are concerned here with entrenched patterns and with how certain behaviors appear to be resistant to change. We are concerned with how pastoral care providers account for change and sameness. Narrative agency, systemic thinking, and intercultural realities may help us to think further.

V

Narrative Agency

Narrative agency is the developing capacity for self-reflexivity—that is to say, the capacity to act in relationship with others and with increased self-conscious awareness. It is the capacity to be guided in the present by body awareness, awareness of past events, and appreciation for how our ancestors struggled amidst the vicissitudes of their time. Narrative agency moves with the awareness that we have inherited a world already carved out by our predecessors. We will make our contribution and achieve an identity within certain social developments, and we will leave a trace within the flow of time. With awareness of certain past developments, one is able to participate in the current flow of things with heightened self-awareness, directivity, and wisdom in co-constructing worlds of meaning. Narrative agency is the capacity to assess critically what is going on, exercise moral choice, make wise decisions among available alternatives, act with compassion while helping to create new opportunities with others, and help shoulder responsibility for the consequences of our actions. In this way narrative agency is one way we account for change—by creating ourselves through time and in relations with others. The social and cultural contexts for narrative agency are important influences on the ways we account for change.

By examining myths of origins, we may construct certain meanings and make sense of why things are as they are. In this light, hope for beneficial change lies in the uncovering of deeper layers of myth and the reemerging of image and holistic approaches to life and work as a sign of regaining balance to centuries of unilateral hegemony and andocentric worldview. It is here that the deconstruction of history of the story of Theseus, Ariadne, and the Minotaur becomes meaningful. Instead of centering our gaze on plots of conquest, the myth itself contains other, perhaps older, layers of meaning that can become blueprints for the complexity of life processes itself, which is the stuff of narrative.

The overturn of matriarchal societies is mirrored in the context of mythology in which classical Greek writers narrate the story of Ariadne and Theseus. Minos, the father of Ariadne, was one of the sons of Zeus who became the father of all gods. He was born to Kronos and hidden by his mother Rhea in the cave of the holy mountain Ida because Kronos tried to devour all of his children in fear of being displaced by them. After Zeus grew up with the help of nymphs and after winning the war of giants and titans, Zeus became the mightiest god of Greek mythology, producing many offspring by coupling with goddesses, nymphs, and princesses. Often, the narrations tell of Zeus' using disguise to get his interests met, even using rape. One of the princesses he abducted and subdued is Europe, daughter of King Agenor of Phoenicia in the Middle East. Zeus approached her in the form of a white bull, and, enchanted by the beauty of the bull, Europe sat on him. Zeus fled with her across the sea, brought her to Crete, and raped her. Europe became the one who gave birth to Minos, Rhadamanthys, and Sarpedon, the kings who reigned in different parts of Crete. It is from her that Europe was named and received its historical roots.

In the historical reading of mythology, all these narratives in Greek mythology witness the overturn of matrifocal and matrilineal societies by patriarchal structures. Here is a legacy of the establishment of unilateral power structures, exploitation, negotiations, and adjustments that led to profound changes in the relationship of men to nature, women, and children. This violent overthrow of matrifocal societies has consequences for narrative agency.

> Around 1500 B.C.E., apparently forced by extensive drought to break out of their traditional patterns of nomadic migration back and forth the trans-Caucasian plains, the Indo-European pastoralists followed their starving herds across the mountains and invaded the settled agrarian matriarchies around the Mediterranean and the Indian subcontinent. They quickly overran the Goddess worshipers they found on the fertile plains and imposed their essentially tragic religious world-views, symbolized by endless generations of gods endlessly overthrowing one another and destroying the earth in the process, on the conquered agriculturalists.[12]

Jeremy Taylor sees the consequences of these historical changes still bleeding through and haunting present-day lives of women and men, especially in their dreams. It is in the dreams (and frequently in the movies and mass media) of women and men that we find these mythic themes being played out.

Systemic Thinking

Systemic thinking is a reflexive process of moving back and forth between memory, present-day events, and social practices. We do this in order to make relevant connections between thought and the kind of worlds we help to create through our activities as we envision a better world. Systemic thinking can be beneficial when groups or collectives engage it in problem-solving activity. If we move back and forth between the familiar and the strange in our experience, then we are able to expand our awareness and evolve our thinking about what is going on in the situations in which we are engaged.

The story of Theseus and Adriadne provides an opportunity for systemic thinking and for finding metaphors that may help us to think at a deeper level about what is going on. The myth begins with recognition of estrangement in the form of a grave injustice and a desire to end suffering and long-standing oppression. According to the main plot, a strong youth, the son of a king, volunteers to risk his life for this task. The hero faces evil, struggles against it until he is victorious, and liberates the people. But he cannot accomplish this alone. He needs Ariadne, without whose help he would be doomed. But this story of sacrifice and liberation is limited. It ends in betrayal and estrangement. Systemic thinking allows us to see this movement and to make connections between this cultural myth and the myths that underlie and guide our strategies for living and our understanding of how and why things change or remain the same.

How does this myth reflect the ordering of gender relations in our societies? Is love fated to be wronged? Are gender relations fated to end in betrayal and estrangement? Are there deeper layers of the truths and myths that guide us? If so, then how do we search for and find them?

Systemic thinking allows us to connect where we are with what we are doing (the connection of thought and behavior). We create the future through our behavior, and whether recognized or not, we reproduce certain established patterns from the past. Our current activity is guided by maps in the mind or certain enduring ways of thinking and being in the world. If maps in the mind are rooted in past stories with tragic outcomes, then are we really free to better our communities and ourselves? How do we change our minds, and how does desired change come?

There are important metaphors in the story that may help. We briefly identify three here: the labyrinth, the ball of string, and the sword. The labyrinth is the path of life that must be traversed. All who enter are challenged. Ariadne brings Theseus resources that can help him to successfully traverse the labyrinth and face evil without being devoured by it. Theseus is to anchor the ball of string to the gate of the labyrinth and make his way through its winding and confusing pathways. She gives him the sword to protect him and to struggle with the evil that lives at the center of the labyrinth. Resources are needed to fight evil. The labyrinth is the journey through life that twists and turns and often leads to challenge or crisis. This may be especially true when traveling the road to peace with justice. Many travelers before Theseus became confused, bewildered, and cynical and lost their way or gave up before they ever reached the center. Others may have made it to the center but were without adequate resources to face the epitome of estrangement in the form of monstrous evil.

If one, like Theseus, is successful with the sword of violence, then is it possible to ever put it down and take up nonviolence and justice as a way to the future? Is it possible to live beyond betrayal and abandonment? If it were not for the ball of string, then even if the slaying of the monster were successful, one would still be hopelessly trapped inside the impersonal walls of the labyrinth. The ball of string is what sustains hope and leads Theseus out of the maze. What then, for us, might be the gate that anchors the thread—the lifeline? What gives us hope that we are being led toward loving relationships? How can we learn to transform our swords into pruning hooks? This myth points to what is at the heart of human estrangement—love betrayed and the death of hope. Here, human estrangement is the religious and meaning context for thinking about change. How is desired change possible?

This tragic ending pushes systemic thinking to search for another layer. This may lead us to Ariadne and Dionysus, who fall in love and had several children together. Several scholars interpret this layer of the myth as narrative. They suggest that narrative is something that has actually happened and is a part of social history. In Heide Goettner-Abendroth's view,[13] mythology as social history goes beyond myth as archetype, expression of ideas, or poetry. Mythology as narrative or social history is the expression of a complex social practice. It becomes a rich source for the construction and functioning of archaic societies. Mythology in this way depicts past practices and worldviews in a typifying way. Comparative studies of the same myth or fairytale resemble the process of an archeological excavation. Remnants of life and belief systems at different times and places become palpable when layer after layer are explored. If we read mythology as social history, then we have a report of events that can lead to transformations in societies, in social practices, and in personal life. Mythology serves as important witness to memories about ancient ways of life that were lost by covering it over with newer social and cultural orderings. In this view, mythology also tells about the overturn of societies by new colonists and the suppression of spiritual traditions by new religious cults.[14] Thus, acknowledgment of the processes of deconstruction and reconstruction in Greek mythology would be important if we are to remain alert to how historical events bleed through and have an impact on thought and the development of social practices, especially in regard to relations of gender, race, and religion today. What bleeds through, itself, becomes a source of change.

Still, there are those who are left out of this understanding of change. Systemic thinking pushes us to connect with even deeper, more inclusive layers of the human story—ones that move beyond estrangement toward a sense of unity that exists as foundation for our diversity. The search for these layers can point us to resources and ways to face monstrous evil, overcome, and heal. Deeper layers of our story may point us to possibilities for desired change in our time.

Intercultural Realities

Theseus and Ariadne belonged to different and conflicting cultures. The Minoan, Crete culture was ancient and matriarchal. The Greek culture, which Theseus represents, is Indogerman and patriarchal. We may see immediately how differences in cultures can lead to conflict between the cultures. But there may be another layer that is less obvious, and that is *intracultural.*

The message of the Theseus and Ariadne story is timeless, and it has a broad application that can be identified. There are stories of oppression within the same culture. German philosopher Heide Goettner-Abendroth has done extensive comparative studies in the history of religions, arts, myths and fairytales, and archeology across continents. According to her research, there have been developing stages of matrilineal and matrifocal societies across the world from the time of the Stone Age up to 3000 B.C.E. Goettner-Abendroth uses the term *matriarchy* to refer to the spiritual and social characteristic of these communities. Matriarchy refers to the Greek term *arche,* meaning the source, the beginning. Matriarchies are tribal societies organized around those who originate in the same womb, the mother. All who originate in the same mother, grandmother, or great-grandmother are important to one another and support one another. Therefore, the relationship between women and men that matters most is the relationship between sisters and brothers. As a-delphphai/oi, from the same womb and source of life, siblings serve their communities, fulfilling diverse tasks according to their environment. The sibling—brother—of a woman also takes care of her children. He is the social father of the children.

The mother's lovers or husbands are regarded as visitors or guests within the tribe. Men stay committed to their mother's tribe even if they live with women from different tribal systems. Matrilineal descent matters because procreation is traceable to mothers. The role of biological fatherhood was not known for a long time and was never regarded as crucial to identity in the community. Important is the survival of all members of a community, not property and rights of offspring. Therefore, all siblings in a tribe exist for one another as brothers and sisters and as cousins of the same grandmother or great-grandmother.[15] Together, they help to bring change.

Matriarchal societies were small communities that lived in relation to the transformations of their environment. Decisions were made by the community on the basis of authority, especially the authority by the oldest women, because they had the deepest experience and knowledge.

Spiritually, the spiraling transformation from death to birth, growth, decline, and death was symbolized in the great goddess who encompassed earth and heaven, universal power, and all life and death (*chtonic* earth goddess in early matriarchies). Later, in developed matriarchies, the goddess was depicted as the threefold moon goddess, representing birth and new life, growth and love, fruitfulness, and death. The mother of the most important clan performed the spiritual representation; at her side, she chose one of her male relatives (son or brother) as her administrator, her consort, and the "king." The matriarchal epoch existed for 4000 years, whereas patriarchal forms of societies began to take over around 3000 to 1500 B.C.E.

An assessment of human change must consider the history of gender relations, cultural traditions, and social conditions that directly influence face-to-face relations. Hence, the possibilities for change are embedded in layers upon layers of experience; not all of the layers are in conscious awareness.

Recently, Ursula visited a matriarchal society in Meghalaya, India. Three tribal traditions live together in matrilineal descent and family structure: the Khasi, the Garo, and the Jaintas. In narrative interviews, Khasi women and men expressed a strong attachment to their ancient tradition, despite certain societal influences that erode. Their strong attachment is best represented by common cultural mores. The most unique is the matrilineal law, which governs lineage and ancestral inheritance through the female line. The experience of self-worth in Khasi women and girls impressed Ursula. Acknowledged as givers and sustainers of family traditions and life, they are supported by Khasi men. The men are responsible fathers and uncles. Men and women together represent the interests of the clans and tribe in their basic democratic structures. Women and men in Meghalaya live according to high moral standards. Indigenous traditions such as those of the Khasi in India remind us that our vision of women and men as siblings by choice is not a pious wish but a wisdom deeply rooted in ancient traditions and cultural practices. They can empower today's struggles against violence and injustice in gender and race relations.

VI

Summary

In this chapter, we examined an old story, a myth of origin, about gender relations in order to see how the old story and its many narrations have been covered over and now bleed through into present-day realities. We argued that change is not a simple matter of the emotions, will, or cognition alone. It is also related to biological structures and deep cultural processes that escape our awareness. Change may come through conflict or by falling in or out of love. It may come through gifts of exchange or result from changes in social position and social structure. Some changes come because older realities bleed through into the present—disrupting familiar ways of thinking and acting—and bring innovation or destruction. The ways in which the old stories bleed through into the present have implications for narrative agency, systemic thinking, and intercultural realities. We cannot intentionally change or heal what we do not understand. We cannot understand the things we do not struggle to change. We seek understanding in order to change what we can and forgive what cannot be changed through effort or years of trying. We must learn to act with greater wisdom, wider justice, and deeper compassion.

We believe that the recovery of certain cultural practices and religious traditions and principles have been subjugated or trivialized by certain preferred and limited patterns of thought in Western societies. The recovery of certain traditions of subjugated knowledge (such as practicing nonviolence, enacting justice, and showing unconditional respect for persons as ends in themselves rather than as means to ends, etc.) may be crucial for human survival and may benefit understanding of the stranger; persons living with disabilities; gays and lesbians; relations between women, men, and children; and groups who live between gender boundaries.

A source of stability or resistance to change may lie in the ways we read or fail to read history and mythologies or fail to learn from lessons that we draw from the past. The lessons we learn and live by shape our perceptions, inform our beliefs, and guide our actions, which, in their turn, help to create and maintain the cultures we live in. Of equal importance is the past that we fail to remember and the lessons we fail to learn. We are also shaped by ignorance.

When immigrants came from Europe with visions and hopes for a new beginning and a new world order, they also brought their own experiences with them as well as their perceptions of white people, of power, and of justice; their notions of insider and outsider; and their ideas on what to do with heretics and pagans, non-white people, gay and lesbian persons, and Moslems and Jews and Catholics. Their past experiences helped to organize the way they adapted to and built the new world. Many Europeans coming to the United States had also experienced the trauma of warfare and failed revolutionary movements in their countries of origin.

In this chapter we also asked how pastoral care providers decide whether someone has changed or not. We note with George Furniss that "Pastoral care has bought heavily into the cultural pluralism and cognitive relativism of modern culture: as caregivers, we see our role as supporting people along the road they have chosen, of being agenda-free, and of being client—(or person) centered."[16] Pastoral care providers are not agenda free. Like everyone else, they are socially located and may better serve help seekers when they puzzle with them over why women and men, families, or organizations are slow to change or repeat the harmful patterns that lead them to seek counseling in the first place. Repetition of violence—rape, for example—is experienced in marriages. Patterns of conflicts repeat through the generations and are manifest in neighborhoods. Patterns of discrimination, duplicity, and deception are slow to change and repeat in institutions and corporations even when promises of change are made. A gap often exists between the willful and urgent cry for *ideal* change versus the *actual* experience of maintaining certain destructive patterns. Strategies for individual and social change have also been stymied by inertia and certain patterns that appear to resist change. The adage, "The more things change, the more they remain the same," appears to be appropriate in many cases. Discussion of the Middle Passage raised the question, Why did the people who fled persecution in European societies in the name of freedom and pursuit of happiness help to establish a slave system and maintain patterns of inequality through broken promises to native people and continued discrimination in the New World?

Therapists, social workers, and pastoral care providers continue to ask and are asked: "Can people change?" The answer is, of course, people are always changing. There are biological forces and enormous historical and contemporary forces at work that bring acknowledged and unacknowledged change. The important question is "Why are we not always able to make the kinds of changes that we would like for ourselves and our communities?"

The context of change is embedded in layers of experience; not all of these layers are in conscious awareness. Therefore, a critical assessment of human change must consider the structure of living systems, cultural myths and traditions, the history of gender relations, and the social conditions that directly influence face-to-face relations.

EXERCISE

How do people change? People rarely change because you tell them to. So how does it happen?

1. Think of all the ways that would cause you to change your behavior or attitude. Make a list.

2. Think of a story to tell in which you changed your behavior or attitude, or you were made (forced) to change.

In threesomes:

1. Exchange information on causes of change in your own experience. Make a group list.

2. Pick a story to share about what caused a change or series of changes in your life. Who were the people most affected by the change? Who were the people least affected? What ethnic, minority, or cultural groups, if any, were affected? What new connections were made, or what lessons, if any, were learned?

3. From the information that was shared in the small group of three, create a roleplay that will draw on your shared experiences and demonstrate some of the challenges, promises, pitfalls, and consequences of changing one's behavior and/or attitude. Consider how these changes help or hinder "doing God's will." What consequences do or did the envisioned change of behavior or attitude have for narrative agency, systemic thinking, and intercultural realities in your situation?

4. Perform the role play with the class or larger group, and lead members in a critical discussion of the issues that are raised.

Death and the Maiden

The Complexity of Trauma and Ways of Healing

The "Tales of the Sibling Clan"—asks what it is like for men and women to establish a covenant with one another, to work out among themselves and without divine intervention their issues of power, and to find a way to live together in community…The spirituality of siblings requires the supreme ability to live with differences in forgiveness and trust.

Peter Pitzele[1]

"Who are my mother and my brothers?"…" Whoever does the will of God is my brother and sister and mother."

—*Mark 3:33, 35*

I

Death and the Maiden is a drama written by Chilean author Ariel Dorfmann.[2] The context is the unstable political situation in Chile after the fall of the brutal dictatorship of General Augusto Pinochet. We selected this drama for our case study as we reflect on the interpersonal issues of trauma and healing within a political context. ⌐ ery case study raises a particular set of issues and questions. We ⸱ve *Death and the Maiden* invites the following important ⸱ons: How does the teacher of pastoral care prepare the student ⸱ess complex issues without losing sight of the individual or ⸱t resources do teachers of pastoral care use to help illuminate the interplay between the personal and the historical, social-political, economic, and ecological contexts? Recently, feminist and liberation theologians have emphasized in their work that the personal is embedded in political contexts; hence, the political is personal, and the personal is political. We will explore the implications of this observation as we explore narrative agency, systemic thinking, and intercultural realities in pastoral care. A discussion about narrative agency will underscore the reality that stories are embedded in social, historical, economic, and political forces. We acknowledge that, at times, a sense of agency can be diminished when powerful forces overwhelm us. Systemic thinking will help us track the reciprocal connections between contexts and individuals as well as note the changes that occur within individuals. "Intercultural realities" is our way of saying that we may encounter cultural contexts that are, or seem, foreign to us. Thus, we arrive at the question, How, then, shall we live?

Death and the Maiden poses a challenge to pastoral care providers in that it places a focus squarely on systemic violence. Pastoral care has been defined primarily in individual terms and as a professional relationship between a help seeker and a help giver. This drama will demonstrate how long-standing patterns of injustice and violation create long-term trauma and irreparable hurt, which can become an integral part of everyday life. Thus, we will see how these long-standing political patterns demand that our definitions and strategies of care be expanded or enhanced to recognize the systemic dimensions of life and living.

The play has three characters: Paulina Salas, her husband Gerardo Escobar, and Dr. Roberto Miranda. The drama unfolds in the main room of Paulina and Gerardo's home. There the history of violence, which permeates every aspect of Chilean society, now determines the interaction between the three characters and the meaning in their personal lives.

Paulina Salas, around forty years old, had worked with her husband, Gerardo Escobar, around forty-five years old, for political change. She was a student activist during the time of Pinochet's dictatorship. One evening she was informed by television that her husband had been- announced head of a committee commissioned to investigate the events of torture during the dictatorship of General Augusto Pinochet. He is hindered in returning by a huge thunderstorm in which they lost power and phone. The husband, Gerardo Escobar, eventually arrives home for dinner with Dr. Roberto

Miranda. As Paulina listens and watches Dr. Miranda in her home, she remembers and is taken back to a time of trauma. Dr. Miranda's way of talking, the way he quotes Nietzsche, and his general manner of behaving makes Paulina suspicious. Was he the one who brutally and repeatedly tortured and raped her when she was a student activist? She begins to believe that the doctor is the one who betrayed and tortured her in the worst possible way. She remembers when she was abducted and tortured because the Pinochet regime had wanted the name of her husband. She remembers that she had been stripped naked, violated, and tortured with electroshocks. After the rape, Dr. Miranda came to attend to her. He promised to help her. Instead, he raped her repeatedly, using her as an object of his own will. She had been humiliated and hurt even more than by the electroshocks. The doctor had even played one of her favorite pieces of music: Schubert's *Death and the Maiden.*

On that night, Paulina had not confessed the name of her husband. She had protected him. But when she had returned home to her husband, she found him in bed with another woman. And now, she finds herself standing in the same room with her torturer and her husband who had betrayed her. She is absolutely clear about what she needs in order to begin healing. Her sense of self-respect, self-agency, and spiritual wholeness must be restored. She needs a confession about the truth of what had happened. She needs an acknowledgment of her suffering from the men who had inflicted it on her. This is exactly what both men in the drama are not willing to give. By using all her wits, strengths, determination, and a gun, she attempts to get what is crucial to restore her inner and outer sense of identity. The confession she receives from Dr. Miranda contains statements such as the following:

> I raped you many times. Fourteen times. I played music. I wanted to soothe you. I was good at first. I fought it hard. No one was so good at fighting as I. I was the last one to have a taste. No one died. I made it easier on them. That's how it started. They needed a doctor. My brother was in the Secret Service. He told me, "Make sure nobody dies." You saw it yourself. You told me you are dirty and I washed you clean. The others said, "You are going to refuse fresh meat, are you?" And I was starting to like it. They laid people out on the table. They flashed on the light. People lying totally helpless, and I didn't have to be nice and I didn't have to seduce them. I

didn't even have to take care of them. I had all the power. I could make them do or say whatever I wanted. I was lost in morbid curiosity. How much can this woman take? More than the other one? How's her sex? Does her sex dry up when you put the current through her? Can she have an orgasm under those circumstances?

O God, I liked being naked. I liked to let my pants down. I liked you knowing what I was going to do. There was bright light. You could not see me. I owned you. I owned all of you. I could hurt you and I could … you and you could not tell me not to. I loved it. I was sorry that it ended. Very sorry that it ended.[3]

Paulina was the maiden who died. True, she survived physically. But her soul, mind, hopes, and trust and the meaning of her life were killed. Even so, she was not broken by the torture. What Paulina needed was the truth from Dr. Miranda, her suspected torturer. The drama leaves open the question of whether or not Dr. Miranda's confession is real or contrived. *Death and the Maiden* deals with the long-term effects of torture and violence on human beings. The drama is mythical and historical in that the themes it deals with are timeless and actual. The fact that violence surrounds us, trauma is complex, and the need for healing is everywhere makes this drama mythical, systemic, and intercultural, and the implications for narrative agency are immediately relevant.

Narrative Agency

Paulina coauthors her own story. She sacrificed herself in order to protect her husband, Geraldo, who then betrayed her. How can healing occur in the relationship between Paulina and Geraldo—that is to say, how can trust be restored? The way Gerardo Escobar can become the real partner of Paulina Salas is to bond with and trust her as she pursues her suspicion about her torturer. Trust becomes a first step to hearing her. He must help and protect her as she did him during the time of her interrogation. He must not be afraid to hear and face the truth of her story, which is also a part of his own. Once Paulina experiences his courage to chose her side and acknowledge her pain, she can let go of her murderous rage. Both Paulina and Gerardo can begin a new phase of grieving and work through their pain. The same possibility exists for Dr. Roberto Miranda, to the degree that he can confess his complicity in the collective and personal violence, acknowledge his responsibility, repent, and make restoration. One of the main problems for Paulina is that even in her own perception she is not certain if her identification of the perpetrator is right. Is Roberto Miranda the one who did the torturing? Not being reinforced in her perception by her husband and facing the denial of the perpetrator are among the most difficult experiences for her.

There are further implications for a sense of narrative agency. Where justice has been long denied and the effects of traumas remain hidden, there will surface a need to deal openly with the trauma and right the wrongs. There will also be strenuous efforts on the part of perpetrators to deny wrongdoing and to disavow any knowledge of it. New identities may be created to cover up the violence.[4] Others may unwittingly become an accomplice in the cover-up. *Death and the Maiden* reveals how a dictatorship created complex public relationships, determined the quality of private lives, and affected an inner sense of self-agency. These interwoven issues (complex external event, private lives, and inner sense of self), in various ways, are manifest through all three of the characters in the drama. *Death and the Maiden* is about a real-life, everyday situation, in that it deals with the long-term effects of betrayal, torture, and violence on human beings. This drama was written in a world marked by differences, unilateral use of power, changing gender roles, and increased violence. It forces the questions, How do we relate to those who have hurt us irreparably or whom we have hurt? What kinds of knowledge need to be unmasked? What information needs to surface? Who is to do this work? Faced with such questions, and in such a context, can we create relationships of safety, holding, and trust while such work is done? Can connections be made and sustained while acknowledging differences in ways of seeing and knowing? In short, how can we encourage a sense of narrative agency?

Systemic Thinking

Systemic thinking is a way of looking at the contexts in which behavior occurs and tracking the reciprocal connections *between* contexts and individuals as well as noting the changes that occur *within* individuals. In this connection, Paulina is faced with a real dilemma. She believes in democracy and fair play. As a student activist, she struggled and risked her life to overturn a dictatorship so that she and others could live in freedom. Now she has the upper hand. In the drama, she has a gun in her hand and orders her husband to tie Dr. Miranda to a chair. She has to decide what to do. She interrogates him because she wants a confession. But should she shoot him? If she does, she will never hear the confession. If she kills him, will she feel that justice has been done? Will the democratic way of life she valiantly struggled for be realized by killing Dr. Miranda, or will she become a murderer, like him? Dr. Miranda's role in the play is ambiguous. Sometimes, you think he is a victim of mistaken identity; at other times, you think that he is guilty, that she has got it right, that he is an animal. His ambiguous role is reflected in her struggle. She has been betrayed and violated. She is alone and understandably bitter, enraged. Her husband unwittingly brings the man she suspects violated her into their home. The temptation to stoop to the tactics of her suspected torturer is great.

The challenge for pastoral care here is in the whole movement of hearing the painful story of victims and then moving perpetrators through the processes of recognition, confession, repentance, and restoration. The events of the drama could happen anywhere. They do occur everywhere. But efforts to acknowledge such events may be resisted. Herein lies a partial challenge for pastoral care and counseling: namely, to make known the subtle connections between personal suffering and public events, especially when people do not want to hear or know. Pastoral counselors may be in an uncommon position to do systemic thinking and reveal the connections between public events, psychic trauma, interpersonal relations, and spiritual direction.

From these ideas we draw the following implications for teaching systemic thinking. The drama *Death and the Maiden* will serve as guide.

First, the teacher or trainer may invite the students to read the drama and reflect on its meaning for them. Then, the teacher may lead the students in a discussion by asking, "What is the problem?" Rather than assuming that the definition of the problem at hand is known or shared, it is important to ask, "What is the problem?" in order to identify and define it. Just as there are different ways of seeing and knowing, there will be different understandings and conflicting definitions of the problem. The different ways of seeing and knowing may later provide alternative approaches to the problematic situation. Hence, it is important to ask what the problem is and uncover the different and many ways of seeing and entering the problematic situation.

Next, the teacher can invite the students to do some background reading about the Chilean situation. Students should be encouraged to identify new questions stimulated by the reading of historical documents and gain perspective on the political context and the author's point of view.

Students can link these new questions with their previous questions about the definition of the problem.

Given what they now know, the students may work in small groups to develop a scenario of the situation that they will role-play. Class members are invited to think about the definition of the situation implied in the particular scenario and how the definition of the situation determines the motives and interaction between the characters as well as the possibilities for healing.

Role-play this situation and think about it from the perspective of each of the individuals in it.

After several role-play situations are presented, the students should be invited to think about the context as a whole. The overall purpose is to enable students to see multiple levels of interaction and meaning and thereby identify alternative approaches and resources for healing. Some resources may already be available in the interaction system and in wider society. Other resources need to be created in order to help transform painful situations.

During this process, another challenge for the teacher and trainer of pastoral care and counseling is to create space and time safe enough to address the pain, shame, anxiety, rage, or denial connected to life stories of traumatization. There may be students or trainees who have been abused themselves and need protection for their own deep emotions, memories, or present experiences. Also, the teacher and trainer need a place where they can take care of their own well-being. Therefore, teaching and training that address violence and traumatization need special care given to the process in order to deal with the emotional involvement of all participants. The development of ritual elements may be helpful because ritualized beginnings and endings help to establish safe boundaries for the time and space needed to process the emotions raised by the role-play. Rituals can consist of small sentences such as "I hear you, sister (or brother)" stated by the whole group after a woman or man has shared her or his feelings. Rituals can include symbols such as a bowl of water for cleansing and refreshing. A stone can be circled in order to contain pain or rage that may then be washed away by water. Rituals are most helpful when they are developed and agreed on by the participants themselves. This is especially important in intercultural[5] settings in which symbols have different meanings for participants from diverse ethnic and spiritual traditions.

Intercultural Realities

Death and the Maiden is a symbolic story. It is one of the key narratives of the present situation in many countries of the world. In October of 1994, we participated in the leadership of an international conference for pastoral counselors, held for the first time in the capital of the Czech Republic, Prague. The theme of the conference, *Changing Values*, indicated the struggles that post-conflict societies are facing, especially the post-socialist countries of Eastern Europe.

We listened to the report of two participants from Papua New Guinea, Biul Kirokim and his interpreter, John. Their village was recently "discovered" by international mining companies. Their natural resources of trees and land were razed, their air and waterways polluted, their customs and traditional way of life irreparably destroyed. New diseases and forms of illness occurred for which they had no remedy. They had to learn to rely on Western medicines, which they could not afford. People became depressed and developed psychological illnesses that were unknown. Their culture was humiliated. An entire people were violated, their land raped, their food source poisoned. Theirs is a trauma of unknown magnitude, and they search for ways to heal.

What are steps to be taken when the trauma is of unknown magnitude? Inviting women and men as speakers and representatives of communities that continue to be exploited and traumatized is one step the intercultural pastoral counseling movement has taken. But even here, questions such as "How did you learn English" and "What kind of food do you eat" were put to Biul Kirokim of Papau New Guinea. Trainers and teachers of counseling from Europe and the United States demonstrated a profound lack of knowledge and interpathy because their questions failed to respond to his life-threatening situation.[6] There was disappointment and anger about our own limitations among some participants of the conference. We became aware of how much we have yet to learn in order to develop models of intercultural counseling in which mutuality of learning and teaching are developed and hurt and anger can be worked through.

What needs to be confronted? Who must do the work? Who needs to tell these kinds of stories? Who needs to hear them? How can relationships of safety, holding, trust, and connections be made in order for victims and perpetrators to be healed? And how do we enable our students to make these connections in ways that empower them to be effective pastoral caregivers and learners in different cultural situations? How do we learn to become siblings —by choice?

One of the presenters, Dr. Jan Urban, a former Czech dissident, offered an answer to these questions. A culture of humiliation and shaming develops where there is personal and systemic violation of the dignity of persons and the effects of trauma are widespread. A culture of humiliation and shaming develops when people are not given space to openly process their experience of trauma after the acute stages of conflict have passed. A culture of humiliation and shaming develops further when public policy promotes amnesia rather than remembering. Public and private amnesia can be as dangerous as the traumatization itself. Jan Urban mentioned *Death and the Maiden* as one of the most important plays that address severe trauma and processes of recovery. This drama was not permitted to be staged in Czech theaters even though its content deals exactly with the experiences that thousands of people have had in the past forty years during and after the war. In this way, public policies promote amnesia when people are not allowed to publicly acknowledge the violence done to them and find appropriate ways to transform their lives. If people do not want to hear or be reminded, then how can they be prepared for the consequences?

Jan Urban named another important challenge: Churches have access to social and political power by being able to speak up publicly. Traumatized persons, as the drama of Paulina's life demonstrates, need the naming of the atrocity that has happened. Not being listened to and believed in when telling the truth is one of the worst experiences for girls or boys when they give signs to adults of being abused. For the speakers of the people in Papua New Guinea, for example, one of the problems they face is the disavowal of the impact of what a Western economy's destruction has done to their ecological and social-spiritual system. Certain companies have produced films that are meant to demonstrate the environmental care provided by these Western companies. They use "scientific research" to legitimate their claims of environmental care. However, the experience of the inhabitants, which contradicts such claims, is denied. Their knowledge is neither heard nor acknowledged in the world's public.

III

Pastoral counselors work between and within the realm of the personal and the political, the private and the public. We listen to personal and political stories like Paulina's when we work with refugees and victims of violence from all parts of the world, including the stranger from afar or the neighbor next door. It is a demanding challenge for a pastoral counselor to listen to stories of torture and respond appropriately to the counselee's or trainee's experiences of not being heard, or stories of violation, frightening dreams, and flashbacks. They become the Paulina Salas in our experiences. We are challenged to help them to express their rage and ambivalence and struggle with shame and isolation. Given this challenge, it is easy for the counselor to feel overwhelmed by this complex reality, to feel helpless, discouraged, incompetent, and burned-out. We might identify strongly with the victim and condemn the perpetrator so that hopelessness or anger seems overwhelming. We might also recognize that there are many issues that we have not yet addressed adequately in our own lives. For example, our response to the amount of abuse toward especially women and children; our own racism, classism, or homophobia; our participation in the structural violence of exploitation of nonwhite societies by White Western culture and economy—these may escape our awareness. How, then, can we meet the challenge to become siblings –by choice?

When working with traumatized women,[7] children, and men, it is important not only to establish safety and reliable connections but also to make transparent the counselor's support of the victim. Counselors may show support of a traumatized victim and increase their understanding of the victim's situation by acting as an advocate. The counselor may do this by helping a rape victim, for example, to gather a support network and by being present at a court hearing. In that way counselors not only show support for counselees, but can enlarge their own understanding of the legal process and of the counselee's personal and political situation. As the problem of traumatization is mainly one of losing the power of decision—the basic sense of self-agency and trust in self, other, and world—it is crucial to address the meaning of life in the process of healing.[8] For example, once the counselor gains an enlarged picture of the counselee's situation, there is greater opportunity to help the counselee find new ways of understanding what happened. The counselor may enable new connections and help birth new meaning in an unfolding story.

It is here that we meet a further special challenge for pastoral counseling. Contemporary models of pastoral care and counseling continue to be under the influence of Western psychology at the expense of engaging in critical reflection on historical experience and ethical traditions as a source of meaning making. Traditional pastoral care used ethical traditions, Bible, theology, reason, and experience as its basis. But with few exceptions, these sources have been neglected. Some of the questions that arise as theological challenges include: How do we use our traditions to address the confrontation with present-day evil, violence, and the traumatization of thousands of women, children, and men? How do we do this theologically and spiritually? Where do we locate our own sources of meaning in our lives in the midst of such violence? What can we learn from the experiences of our ancestors? What do biblical symbols—such as the phrases "the freedom to which Christ has liberated us," "do the will of God," and "brothers and sisters"—mean to us? How do we listen to the voices expressed by women and men of diverse religious traditions? They question the androcentric metaphors and paradigms in which the Christian message of healing and restoration has been cast. Those who suffer point to the need for new interpretations that make sense of their experiences and offer hope for everyone. How do we communicate our own moral vision and resources and committed actions in ways that respect the otherness of others and, at the same time, create safe space for steps towards healing and creativity? How can we teach others in a way that makes it a learning experience empowering for all participants? Answering these questions by the way we live can give direction to how we become siblings by choice.

IV

Death and the Maiden moved both of us deeply. We identified with the victim's rage and uncompromising desire for revenge to balance the scale of justice and to make the perpetrators pay –in full. Why should they be let off? It brought up memories of our own pains and wishes to be acknowledged in our experiences of abandonment, rejection, and devaluation. But the drama must also permit us to identify with those situations in which we have oppressed, violated, or figured into the trauma of others. To recognize this more complex level of trauma can lead to denial or to reconciliation and to healing. It can release energies of hope when emerging narratives are enlarged and incorporate our idealized self as well as our shameful self. A more complex understanding of trauma can offer metaphors of transformation that enable us to connect the violence that is within with the brutal, systemic violence that comes from without. Both may be denied. Both possibilities present us with opportunities to re-envision the meaning of care in a world of increased violence, where political change and upheaval are creating new forms of trauma and affiliations. Ours is a changing world, pushed by global developments, technological innovations, and uneven growth, with deeper divisions between the wealthy and the poor. We are challenged to raise anew the question, Who is my mother, my sister, and my brother? We have much to learn from the questions and the answers, especially in contexts of worldwide economic and social change. Pastoral caregivers are further challenged to fashion creative responses to violence, to see and make the connections between personal suffering and political activity—especially where long-standing patterns of injustice and violation contribute to long-term trauma and irreparable hurt.

There is a prophetic dimension to this challenge. It is to make known the subtle connections between personal suffering and public events, especially where people do not want to hear or be reminded of their past. Pastoral caregivers are challenged to find or create a role in situations where people who refuse to heed warning signs will, nevertheless, be unable to escape the consequences of their refusals. This is analogous to the young smoker who ignores the warning signs and refuses to stop. Such a person may soon be faced with the consequences of lung cancer and early death. She and he may never acknowledge their contribution to all the others affected by their behavior. We are challenged to find courage and skill to confront the perpetrators' denials of violations and to find compassion sufficient to enable them to take responsibility for the consequences of their actions. This means that pastoral caregivers will be challenged to hear painful stories and learn to move perpetrators through the processes of recognition, confession, repentance, and restoration. And what about forgiveness? How do we deal with the perpetrators' confessions and repentance? Are there deeds so horrendous that forgiveness is impossible? In the process we too must learn to recognize our limitations and the complex levels of trauma that incorporate both our idealized and shameful selves.

EXERCISE

In this chapter on *Death and the Maiden*, the focus was on the complex nature of trauma and a search for ways of healing. Where pastoral care has been defined primarily in terms of personal healing or as one-on-one talk therapy, systemic connections with attention to long-standing patterns of injustice and violation may be difficult to assess. Long-standing patterns of injustice and violation help to create long-term suffering for individuals and groups. We may not see how systemic forces, oppressive patterns, long-term political trauma, and irreparable hurt can become an integral part of a person's everyday life. We present a vignette, with permission, from a real-life situation below. Names have been changed to protect the real identities of persons. After reading the vignette, we will ask you to identify the systemic violence and pattern(s) of long-term trauma that affect the actors in different ways and make it difficult for them to become siblings by choice.

After years of trying, Joan had finally achieved her goal of changing her male name (John) to the one she wanted. She received a notice from the local post office to come and pick up the envelope that contained the official documents that permitted her to change her name and gender identity. This included a new passport. Joan was excited and full of hope. Finally, her prayers and persistent efforts to live publicly as a woman were beginning to pay off. She took her bicycle and rode to the post office as fast as she could. When she arrived, the woman clerk asked Joan for her ID card. Joan gave it to her. Of course, Joan's ID still carried her male name, John. The clerk said, "I am sorry, I cannot give the envelope to you; it is addressed to Joan, but your ID is not the same—it shows 'John.'" Joan tried to explain to her that in the very envelope the clerk was holding were her (Joan's) documents that allowed for the name change. The clerk was cold and distant in her response: "I cannot let you open the envelope because you do not have the proper ID. I am sorry!" Joan was devastated! She protested loudly, but to no avail. Joan thought that she would go crazy. The identity she had long struggled for was sealed in an envelope that she could not have. Joan returned home without the documents that would free her to live life as she wanted.

1. Write about the systemic forces and oppressive patterns that were operating in this situation. What were the consequences for

narrative agency for Joan and for the clerk? How would systemic thinking about this situation be helpful?

2. Meet with two other classmates to discuss your assessment of this situation, where you agree and disagree.

3. Discuss what you imagine would happen if Joan and the clerk were able to come together as siblings by choice. What would be the consequences for them: What would be the consequences for Joan, for the clerk, and for the way business is conducted around these and similar issues at the post office? What would be the role of pastoral care in this process?

Complexity and Simplicity in Pastoral Care

The Case of Forgiveness

The Old Coventry Cathedral was destroyed during an air raid Thursday, 14 November 1940. A few days after the bombing, two irregular pieces of the oak roof beams—charred but still solid for lengths of 12 feet and 8 feet respectively were tied together by wire…and set up at the east end of the Ruins. Beneath the Charred Cross and carved on the stone altar in the sanctuary of the Ruins are the words "FATHER FORGIVE"[1]

If you, O LORD, should mark iniquities,
Lord, who could stand?
But there is forgiveness with you.

Psalm 130:3–4a

"Forgive us our debts,
as we also have forgiven our debtors."

Matthew 6:12

Introduction

This chapter is about forgiveness and pastoral care in the context of systemic oppression and certain intercultural realities. Systemic oppression includes, but is not limited to, institutionalized racism, collective violence, rape, torture, persecution, and historical discrimination. It may result in long-term suffering, demoralization, hopelessness, and, possibly, death. The spiritual dimension of systemic oppression must also be recognized. It suggests that we have a relationship to God *and* to one another. Each violation of a living being, be it physical, psychical, emotional, or by social mistreatment, affects the divine-human relationship and is destroying the integrity of that being, her or his wholeness. This constitutes a spiritual problem and one that the practice of pastoral counseling ought to address.

We believe that one of the fundamental underlying issues of pastoral care and counseling in various cultures has to do with issues of forgiveness. As such, we are not treating any one specific culture, but a dynamic that underlies pastoral care and counseling in many different cultures. Forgiveness defines a basic challenge worldwide for pastoral care and counseling.

In his drama *Death and the Maiden*, Ariel Dorfmann raised the question, Is forgiveness really possible in the aftermath of rape and extreme experiences of torture? Forgiveness is not simply a matter of forgetfulness, repression, or suppression. Forgiveness suggests a very complex relationship between victims, perpetrator, and the system of persecution when placed in the context of torture or systemic oppression. There are several levels of relationship in a complex system of persecution. They include the relationship: (a) between the victim and the one who directly inflicts pain; (b) between the agents of the pain and their positions in the line of command; (c) between the agents and the system of persecution; (d) among the bureaucrats who maintain systems of torture; (e) among all who are in positions of responsibility, even if they are far removed from carrying out the torture; (f) among all in the host society that tolerates it; (g) between the victim and her- or himself, and the belief and trust of the god within; and (h) between the victim and the "witness," the one who listens to and acknowledges the experience of the traumatized individual(s). The witness encourages the human capacity for resiliency and enables and supports the injured person through a healing process. Forgiveness may entail all these levels of relationships. Hence, forgiveness is not a simple matter of letting go or of repression.

A few years ago, on a flight back to San Francisco from Denver, Archie and his seat partner got into a conversation about forgiveness. His seat partner was a Jewish medical doctor and philosopher. He was born in Vienna in the early 1940s and left for the United States just before the Nazis took control. He commented that the Christian concept of forgiveness made no sense to him. After learning about Auschwitz, it was impossible for him to believe in or pray to a personal god. He appeared a bit agitated as he said this. He threw his hands in a downward direction as if in disgust or to denounce something. He said, "I am not unreligious. I am just a-religious or non-religious." He repeated that "forgiveness" did not make philosophical sense to him. He then gave the following statements as an illustration of his thinking.

If ten years ago a tragic event happened and the perpetrators were aware of their part in it but were not asking or seeking forgiveness, then what is the point of saying, "I forgive you"?

If ten years ago a tragic event happened and the perpetrators were not aware of their part in it and were not asking or seeking forgiveness, then what is the point of saying, "I forgive you"?

If ten years ago a tragic event happened and the perpetrators were asking forgiveness because they were a part of the general history (i.e., German guilt in the Nazi atrocities), but those seeking forgiveness never participated in specific acts of torture and extermination, then what is the point of the victim's saying, "I forgive you"? How does this help the victim?

If ten years ago a tragic event happened and the perpetrators were asking or seeking forgiveness, but they were not doing anything to correct the behaviors that led to the tragic events in the first place, then they are basically the same people today and would do the same again should similar circumstances materialize. What good does it do for the victims to say, "I forgive you"?

If ten years ago the perpetrator was asking or seeking forgiveness and has been doing things to correct the behaviors that led to the first tragic event, then the perpetrator has already changed and is not the same person today. What is the point of the victim's saying to the changed perpetrator, "I forgive you," when the person who is seeking forgiveness today is not the same person who committed the tragedy ten years earlier?

Archie's seat companion then said, "You see...forgiveness makes no philosophical sense to me." Archie did not challenge him. Rather, he listened respectfully to his (almost) seventy-year-old seat partner who narrowly escaped being a victim of the Nazis in Vienna. He could be right if forgiveness were solely a matter of cognition that could be expressed in a set of statements with logic and linear thought processes. But forgiveness is much more complex, and as we have already noted, it entails many different levels—the emotional, psychological, spiritual, intimate relational, communal, and political.

Primo Levi describes the image of the "drowned" in his book *Survival in Auschwitz*. The drowned is "an emaciated man, with head dropped and shoulders curved, on whose face and in whose eyes not a trace of a thought is to be seen."[2]

Such a person has been reduced to silence by forces of oppression from without and from within. Forgiveness is improbable for persons in such a state of extreme demoralization. Although Levi is describing the faces he saw in a Nazi death camp, his composite image is representative of the cumulative forces of human evil etched on the tortured of our time. The drowned are both sign and symbol of those who have lost the capacity for anger, protest, or hate. They are the women, men, and children who "suffer and drag themselves along in an opaque intimate solitude, and in solitude they die or disappear, without leaving a trace in anyone's memory."[3] Archie's seat partner did not describe this extreme situation of systemic oppression and improbable forgiveness, but Archie believed he could have. In situations of collective violence where human suffering is immeasurable, this level of trauma is horrifyingly normal. How is forgiveness possible?

We have thought about Archie's seat partner's complex way of framing the issue of forgiveness. He did not make it a simple matter. Indeed, he said that it was impossible to believe in the idea of forgiveness as a concept related to justice and as a viable way to be human. His analysis was from the point of view of the victim whose act of forgiveness would release the perpetrator from responsibility and guilt. It would not address the shame and humiliation of the victim or bring justice. Hence, forgiveness is a meaningless gesture, he claimed. What sense does it make for the victim to forgive when perpetrators are not seeking it, lack comprehension of their deeds, or are essentially the same people today and would do the same if the opportunity were to present itself again?

We shall consider the relevance of these questions and ideas of forgiveness by drawing on vignettes from different cultural and international contexts. Ursula will reflect on her experiences in Germany as therapist and professor of pastoral theology and care. Archie will reflect on experiences in Great Britain and the United States. The vignettes below will add dimension to the questions of forgiveness as we consider it across different cultures.

Vignette 1: Dresden: Racism, Violence, and Forgiveness?

In her introductory class on theory and practice of pastoral care and counseling, Ursula asks her students to take a narrative approach and interview a person or a family, and then report on the interview in class. Students are asked to listen to the life-story and evaluate it by asking for indications of dominating knowledge, underprivileged knowledge, preferred ways of living, and sources of power in their own lives.

One student, whom we shall call K., interviewed an old man, whom we shall call Mr. F. Mr. F. had recently returned to Dresden from Russia. This is his life story.

Mr. F. was a youngster when the Nazis took over in Germany. One law after another was introduced. These laws diminished the rights of certain persons. Those especially affected were Jews, homosexuals, Sinti, Roma, and psychiatric patients. The latter were labeled, "Life not worthy to live." The people of Dresden stood by. They did not protest or intervene as the rights of these citizens were diminished. One of the laws promoted racism by demanding that every German family trace its family of origin for several generations and show proof of its roots in the Arian race.

Mr. F.'s family originally came from Rumania. His mother was able to trace back her origins according to the law. His father could not find the ethnic and racial roots of his relatives. Thus, a Nazi administration officer inscribed on his passport, "Jew!" This fateful act changed his life forever. It led to a series of events that seem unbelievable and had disastrous consequences for his entire family. They were forcefully deported to Poland together with many other Jewish families from Dresden. There, they were brought to the Ghetto in Warsaw. It had been emptied when Polish Jews were sent to concentration camps and murdered. The new arrivals were told that they would get their belongings by train. Their friends managed to send their belongings. But when the train arrived at Warsaw, the Nazis bombed the city that very night. Their belongings were destroyed. While in Warsaw, Mr. F. heard about the possibility of work in the USSR. This was appealing. He was young and adventurous. He applied and was transferred to the Soviet Union, where he was employed. He worked hard. But during the war he was under suspicion of being a German spy. The Soviets put him in jail for several years. When he got out of jail, he was transferred to another region and started a new life.

Anti-Semitism was soon on the rise again. He became the object of persecution, having the *J* already inscribed on his passport. He was jailed once again for many years. He was eventually released and once again started a new life. He married, established a new home, and had a family. He maintained a friendly disposition. He got to know tourists and visitors from East Germany and had good conversations with them. When East and West Germany were reunited in 1989–1990, a new law encouraged former German Jews to return to Germany from Russia. Returning Jews were promised compensation. He responded positively to this encouragement to return to his homeland. But new problems arose around his identity when he returned to Dresden, where he was born. Unwittingly, he was able to convince the post-Nazi administration that he never was Jewish in the first place and that his inscription as a Jew was due to Nazi terror. The new Dresden administration saw in this a new opportunity and now conveniently withholds his compensation because he is not recognized as a returning Jew. He now struggles to survive with very little money and in an economy that has grown very expensive. He cannot afford the rising cost of housing and the general increase in the cost of living.

This vignette about systemic oppression mirrors how racism, militarism, economic interests, and violation of human rights were intertwined. The student found Mr. F. to be a lively, cheerful man who still invests in life. He has many contacts and is able to share his story with others. In spite of systemic forms of injustice such as racism; violence; separation from his father and mother, friends, and families; the trauma of several dislocations; and long years of innocent imprisonment, he somehow remains buoyant. He appreciated the willingness of the student to listen to him without much interruption. She became a witness and gave voice to his experience and his family's experience of systemic and systematic racism, violence, and injustice.

This vignette leads to many questions about forgiveness. If forgiveness presupposes repentance, then who is to repent? How can forgiveness be meaningful in this situation? We extend the questions raised by the Jewish doctor Archie met on his plane ride. If no one has acknowledged wrongdoing, apologized, or offered or made restitution, then what sense does forgiveness make? Who can forgive in a life journey where so many people participated in different acts and levels of violence, injustice, and racism, knowingly and unknowingly? What happens when injustice is inscribed and experienced in many ways at different times and places? Injustice becomes a characteristic way of life, inscribed on society itself. This vignette suggests that systemic injustice and racism are everywhere. The good in life is intertwined with evil and affects victims and perpetrators disproportionately—regardless of ethnicity, personal attributes, or political background.

Vignette 2: Dresden: Sexism, Power, and Justice—An Internationally Challenging Problem

A student/social worker from Dresden narrated her experience with a married sixty-five-year-old woman who came to a local women's shelter. The sixty-five-year-old woman had been married fifty years and lived in a village with her husband. The couple owned a large house. The husband, now seventy-three, had been mayor of a neighboring village. Jealousy played a big role in their relationship. The wife had been suffering his abuse for the past fifteen years. The situation worsened and came to a head when he forced her to drive to a place where he wanted to convict her of an alleged offense. But he was unable to do so. The husband was not able to "prove" his wife's guilt. She was innocent. On the way home he made her leave the car. She walked home alone. Upon arrival she discovered that he had locked all the doors to the house. She sought help from a neighbor who, in turn, brought her to the women's shelter. The sixty-five-year-old woman told the student/social worker that her husband had weapons in the house. Because she did not bring any clothes with her to the shelter, it was necessary to go to her home under police escort to get her clothes. Police escort to the house of the abused woman was arranged. Both systems—the women's shelter and the local police—planned everything. Yet there was another police officer from another city involved. He had not been a part of the conversation that led to the plan between the women's shelter and local police. The special task force of the police officer from the other city was to search for the weapons. The husband was held in the police car in order to protect the wife and the social worker. The wife was told to get the most necessary things and return from the house so that a weapons search could be conducted. It was here that differing interests collided. The police officer that was commanding the weapons search spoke harsh and threatening words to the social worker. The officer felt that the woman was taking too long to gather her things, and he wanted to begin the weapons search right away. The social worker felt caught in the middle of the woman's need to gather her belongings and the harsh words from the police officer. The social worker felt overwhelmed. She grew anxious, paralyzed, and unable to act according to her professional wishes.

What was going on? The social worker/student felt disrespect from the police officer and wondered how she could deal differently and professionally in the future with a similar situation. Why was she so paralyzed?

Where is the issue of forgiveness in this situation? There were implicit issues of whether to forgive or to withhold forgiveness. Three general areas that are relevant to the vignette include: (1) the wife's relationship with herself and with her future. It will be important for her to gain help in clarifying her relationship with herself and with her life of suffering abuse, living with weapons in the home, deciding where "home" will be, and planning what to do next. (2) The gender and power issues of professional abuse, the women's shelter, and the harsh treatment of the social worker by police authority. How can professional women who run a shelter for abused women ask male members of the police department to apologize? Are professional women who run a shelter expected to forgive automatically other professionals who treat them disrespectfully? If no wrongdoing is acknowledged by the commanding police officer, would forgiveness have any meaning? (3) The role of witness that the social worker played by hearing the sixty-five-year-old woman's experience of abuse, and the role of witness played by the group of students who observed and acknowledged the painful experience of their sister student. Can she forgive herself for feeling professionally "paralyzed"?

Vignette 3: The United Kingdom: Stephen Lawrence: An Example of Systemic Oppression

On April 22, 1993, a young Black teenager, Stephen Lawrence, was murdered while waiting with a friend, Duwayne Brooks, for a bus in southeast London. A gang of five White youth approached, assaulted them with racial slurs, and attacked Stephen and his friend. Duwayne Brooks managed to escape, but Stephen Lawrence was knocked to the ground, kicked, and beaten. He died from his injuries. His murderers were never charged for the murder. The Metropolitan Police's investigation into the murder of Stephen Lawrence was described by a High Court Judge as fundamentally flawed and marred by a combination of professional incompetence, institutional racism, and a failure of leadership by senior officers. Little would have been done about the murder or the police investigation had it not been for the outcry of the Black community, the quest for justice, the support of the family's minister, and the efforts of Stephen Lawrence's parents, who pressed for an investigation of the police's handling of their son's murder. As a result of their persistent effort and the investigation of High Court Judge Sir William Macpherson, a report was issued. It called for widespread reform in government and social institutions. It defined racism as "the collective failure of an organization to provide an appropriate and professional service to people because of their colour, culture or ethnic origin. It can be seen or detected in processes, attitudes and behavior which amount to discrimination through unwitting prejudice, ignorance, thoughtlessness and racist stereotyping which disadvantage minority ethnic people."[4] Six years later, *The Guardian* newspaper reported, "Any parent faced with the death of their son in such circumstances would have been devastated. But for Stephen's parents, Doreen and Neville Lawrence, their sense of despair has been compounded by the failure of the criminal justice system to deliver them justice to secure the conviction of those responsible."[5]

The unprovoked and racist attack that lead to Stephen Lawrence's death is not an isolated or singular event. It is a part of the Black experience in Britain and an established way of life. Racism can be "seen or detected in processes, attitudes and behavior" that result in harm to non-White people.

Here is another example. On June 4, 2000, fourteen-year-old Christina was the victim of a racist attack by a gang of four White youth near her home. She lived with her widowed father, Jan Marthin Pasalbessy, age forty-eight, a former merchant seaman from Indonesia. Because of Christina's head injuries from the attack, her father took her to the nearby hospital. There Christina and her father ran into members of the same group who attacked her. This time they verbally attacked Mr. Pasalbessy. According to news reports, they called him "Black bastard" and punched and kicked him until he fell to the ground. They continued the attack while his daughter, Christina, looked on helplessly. Mr. Pasalbessy died of injuries the next day, leaving his daughter an orphan. The gang who attacked Mr. Pasalbessy were all convicted of his murder. At the trial the prosecution told the court that the attack on Mr. Pasalbessy was unprovoked, gratuitous violence.[6] "The murder of Christina's father was one of at least eight killings in Britain with a racist element since the publication two years ago of Sir

William Macpherson's ground-breaking report into the botched Stephen Lawrence murder inquiry."[7]

Racism is systemic—an entrenched, institutionalized pattern that will be with us for a long time to come. Given this, what does forgiveness mean for the individual, for society, and for our sense of justice? It seems improbable that forgiveness of the perpetrators by the victim's survivors will bridge the gap between them, especially where the perpetrators have not admitted to any wrongdoing and are not seeking forgiveness. How can Stephen Lawrence's parents forgive when no one has confessed or been held responsible? How can fourteen-year-old Christina forgive those who attacked her and then took her father's life, leaving her an orphan? Was there no one at the hospital to witness this event or who could have restrained the attackers? How can malicious acts and institutionalized patterns of racism be forgiven?

Vignette #4: The United States: Racism, Force and Forgiveness?

It was the counseling session just after the Fourth of July holiday weekend. My counselee was a Black man in his early twenties. He appeared a bit agitated as he entered my office. He sat down and blurted out the phrase, "This was a rough weekend!" "What happened?" I asked. It was Saturday night, and he was returning home from a gig in San Francisco. He was a musician, and his jazz combo had just finished playing for a dance. After he had gotten off the underground train on his way home, police cars converged on him. One officer forcefully pushed him to the ground and held a cocked pistol to the back of his head, saying, "I know you are the one who did it." My client asked, "Did what? What are you talking about?" He tried to explain where he had been and that he was heading home from work. He had an underground train ticket to verify his story. A police officer said in reply that anyone could grab an underground train stub for an alibi. He was shoved into the police car and jailed.

A store had been robbed, unknown to my counselee. The storeowner came to the police station and identified my counselee as the one who had robbed his store. My counselee was roughed up. He called a friend and asked him to go to his bank and get out a large sum of money for his bail. The friend did this, and my counselee was released. After examining the film of the robbery taken by the camera in the store, the police concluded that my counselee was not the one who had committed the robbery. My counselee asked for the return of his moneys. He was told that it was not possible. He went to his attorney, who informed him that police always make mistakes like that. He would just have to get over it and chalk it up as one of those experiences in life that happens.

This was not the first harsh encounter my counselee had had with the police. This experience reflects a typical experience of young Black men with the law and the so-called justice system. They are expected to grin and bear it, but not to retaliate when they are wrongfully accused and harshly handled. My counselee said, "I understand how Rodney King[8] felt about those police officers who beat him." Rodney King was another Black man who was beaten by the police during his arrest. The acquittal of police who had arrested him ignited rioting in Los Angeles, California.

This experience of brutal police force is commonplace for young Black men. It may be viewed as an incident of racial profiling. Racial profiling is defined here as the practice by police to stop motorists or a pedestrian and interrogate them because they appear to be a member of a racial or ethnic group that officers believe are more likely than others to commit certain types of crimes. This practice has been enforced for a long time and is viewed as widespread in the United States and in Britain, especially among young Black men.

Is forgiveness relevant to this situation of racial profiling and injustice? Archie's counselee was falsely accused and forcefully arrested. When he turned to his attorney, a representative (or witness) of the justice system, for help, he was told to "forget about it, overlook the offense, and get on with the rest of your life." Here, social and political issues of racial injustice were interwoven with traumatic and emotional experience. The victim was made to pay twice (once when he was falsely accused, forced to the ground, and jailed, and again when he posted bail to gain his freedom). His perpetrators were never held accountable. They never apologized. They were not seeking forgiveness. They were not interested in making restitution. They were merely going about their job. What sense does forgiveness make in the context of this experience?

We have asked many questions about forgiveness regarding when and where it is relevant. All of the above vignettes raise forgiveness issues. If no one has acknowledged wrongdoing, apologized, repented, or offered or made restitution, then what sense does forgiveness make? Who can forgive in a life journey in which many people have participated in different acts and levels of violence, injustice, and racism, knowingly and unknowingly? Holocaust survivors, fifty years after the horrendous events, may or may not be able to forgive. But their grandchildren, who never experienced the atrocities firsthand, are not in the position to forgive either. They were not victims and never knew the perpetrators. How can past collective violence and institutionalized patterns of racism be forgiven? How can women with little power (as in a shelter for women) forgive men with much greater power (police authority)? The vignettes come from societies that are influenced by Western and Judeo-Christian values. There are in these societies (Germany, the United Kingdom, and the United States) a generally shared and Christianized democratic ethic that people should love, forgive, and bear one another's burdens. This ethic may also be vaguely stated in the golden rule: "Do unto others as you want them to do unto you." It underlies a sense of fair play or justice. There are different conditions for the expression of this ethic, different interpretations of what this may mean and variations within each of the societies, and different interpretations of who is included in neighbor love and who is not. Not everyone accepts this ethic. Christianity is not the only force that shapes a complex value system in each of these societies. There are other influences and interests, such as nation building and recovery from war experiences, cultural development, the spirit of capitalism and socialism, equality. The history and infrastructure of these societies are very different from one another. And so goes the experience of forgiveness. Experience with abuse, the degree of trauma, and demoralization will influence understandings of forgiveness and whether or not one can or ought to forgive. Forgiveness or withholding forgiveness will vary and depend on whether or not one is able to resolve mistrust, despair, and demoralization and begin to build a new life. These capacities will depend on the individual's beliefs and capacity for resiliency and available therapeutic resources that will vary in different cultural contexts. What role can spirituality, our sacred texts, and theology play?

Forgiveness: A Biblical Perspective

The Judeo-Christian tradition professes a belief in a forgiving God. The Old Testament describes those in covenant with God and details their faithlessness, rebellion, disobedience, repentance, and God's offer to deliver them. The backdrop for this cycle is God's faithfulness; God is ever ready to forgive. Forgiveness involves sorrow for offenses committed, repentance, and intention to live an upright life. If there is no sorrow, repentance, or change, then there is no divine pardon. "Even though a man pays another whom he has insulted, he is not forgiven by God, until he seeks forgiveness from the man he has insulted. That man, if he does not forgive the other, is called merciless."[9] Repentance and forgiveness become ways for God to cleanse the people from all sins committed against God and one another. In the New Testament, the word *aphesis* (forgiveness) is almost always that of God.[10] To this extent, the concept is the same as that in the Old Testament. But in the New Testament, there is a new and specifically Christian feature evident. The community realizes that it has to receive from God the forgiveness that is offered through the saving act of Jesus Christ.[11]

Although the word *aphesis* enjoys secular usage as well, in the New Testament the word is used thirty-six times, always meaning pardon for sins, as if this were a technical term reserved for religious use.[12] "It first occurs on the lips of Zechariah in his description of the goal of John the Baptist's ministry, namely to give to the people the knowledge of salvation through the forgiveness of their sins."[13] Baptism is a means of realizing this conversion, and its goal is a washing, the remission or forgiveness of sins.[14] In the covenant sealed by Jesus with the institution of the eucharist, the new covenant is shed for the remission of sins.[15] Thus, *aphesis* is the fundamental element of redemptive work. It is connected with pardon, sanctification, and salvation.[16] In the preaching of Peter at Pentecost and throughout the book of Acts, this forgiveness depends on faith in the person and power of Jesus; it is universal, so that everyone can benefit from it.[17] God's power of forgiveness is creative and ongoing. We are continually offered the possibility or opportunity to forgive or to withhold forgiveness.

In the synoptic gospels this is a forgiveness to which humanity is constantly referred; it is a forgiveness that can be received as long as one is willing to forgive others (Mt. 6:12, 14; 18:21–35; Lk. 17:3; Mk. 11:25).[18] Derived from the central theme of the oneness of God and humankind, and the inseparability of loving both God and neighbor, is the understanding that forgiveness given by God and to others are intimately related. "Forgive us our debts, as we also have forgiven our debtors. And do not bring us to the time of trial, but rescue us from the evil one. For if you forgive others their trespasses, your heavenly Father will also forgive you; but if you do not forgive others, neither will your Father forgive your trespasses"(Mt. 6:12–15).

It is this imperative "to forgive" that is potentially destructive and dangerous in a diverse and complex world. When the understanding of forgiveness is to give unconditional pardon, to forget, to repress, to overlook an injury, to condone, or to excuse the perpetrator from responsibility, then forgiveness is shallow, premature, and potentially harmful to the one forgiving. This form of premature forgiveness (or unconditional pardon) is what Archie's seat partner referred to when he said, "If ten years ago a tragic event happened and the perpetrators were aware of their part in it but were not asking or seeking forgiveness, then what is the point of saying, 'I forgive you'? Or if they were asking or seeking forgiveness, but they were not doing anything to correct the behaviors that led to the tragic events in the first place, then they are basically the same people today and would do the same again should similar circumstances materialize. What good does it do for the victims to say, 'I forgive you'?" To require forgiveness under these circumstances is premature and destructive. On the one hand, it is destructive because it traps the victim in a false sense of guilt and shame. This imperative to forgive is destructive when it serves to devalue the victim, fails to recognize her or his integrity, and contributes to her or his humiliation and lack of self-esteem. It may also be a destructive form of rationalization—that is, "They did not intend to harm me," or "I was wrong to provoke them." It is a destructive form of rationalization when it serves as a defense against self-blame, anger, depression, and feelings of aggression or as a doomed attempt to combat hopelessness. On the other hand, it is destructive when it serves to enshrine the unrepentant perpetrators in self-righteous attitudes, legitimate their harmful behavior, and support its repetition. When this happens, it furthers oppressive practices and weakens, if not helps to destroy, the social fabric of which we are all a part.

True, there may be specific situations in which an injured party might say "I forgive you" *before* wrongdoing has been admitted. The source of injury may be an event, or it may be an agent. In such instances, the party who says "I forgive you" is not under the "imperative to forgive" in the sense that we have talked about it above. They are exercising choice. The injured party may have come to a decision about the injury or worked it through and is ready "to let it go," "release" themselves from it, or "let it be" and "leave." He or she may have mourned the injury and have recognized his or her own need to move forward with his or her own life. To find an acceptable way to move forward implies the work of meaning integration and overcoming the separation within the self that the injury may have helped to create. Where a specific agent is involved, he or she may recognize that the perpetrator is incapable of or may never admit to having done wrong. But the injured party is ready to move on. Readiness to move on is a sign of self-growth and a form of self-release, rather than a pardon of the perpetrator. The unrepentant perpetrator is still accountable for his or her behavior. The injured party, however, may have worked through the meaning of the injury and is ready for something new.

The Christian imperative to "forgive" (i.e., "pardon") must be understood within the context of repentance, divine justice, and mercy. Both repentance and mature forgiveness are acknowledgements that we live in an imperfect world and that human beings commit grievous errors. When they regret such errors, repent, and seek amendment of life, then meaning in life is redeemed. To repent, seek forgiveness, and work to amend life is a way to bring renewal and healing, insight, greater freedom, and wider justice into situations that might otherwise become enshrined in self-righteous attitudes, repetition of harmful behavior, and oppression. Repentance and mature forgiveness can help strengthen the social fabric, the links between people, and the ties that bind them.

Pastoral care providers recognize that repentance and forgiveness can be the means through which injured relationships can be restored. It can be experienced as the creative power of God released and clothed in the speech and activity of the common people. The difficult challenge, then, in every human encounter is to come to the decision about whether to forgive or withhold forgiveness, to acknowledge the depth of our involvements and injuries, and to stand before God in faith and openness to the transforming power of forgiveness. This is a difficult challenge, because human forgiveness may not be possible or desirable in all situations, especially in situations of extreme prejudice where wrongdoing has not been acknowledged, forgiveness is not being sought, and the offender is not seeking peace with justice. Pastoral caregivers may ask: When is the offering of forgiveness premature? When is it not warranted? Under what conditions is forgiveness destructive? What is mature forgiveness?

It is when forgiveness is seen in relationship to power, love, and justice that it is mature. It is healthy, holistic, and potentially redemptive when it is mature. This kind of forgiveness is necessary for spiritual and psychological development. It is related to the important processes of recognizing the injury, appropriately expressing anger, seeking information, and finding appropriate resolution. For those who hold fast to a tradition that asks that they forgive, helping them to see forgiveness in this new and expanded light can itself be a redemptive process.

For the purposes of this chapter, we define "forgiveness" as the redemptive activity of the Divine that works in and through human activity. It can be a creative form of release when it emerges from awareness of our own ongoing experiences with forgiveness, our ongoing human capacity for injuring others and being injured by them (intentionally or unintentionally). Mature forgiveness is manifest through a process of discernment whereby responsible forms of power are recognized and one comes to decide how to hold others and oneself accountable. Mature forgiveness requires that justice with compassion is served, healing is possible, and our lives can move forward with integrity and faith in God's redemptive purposes.

Theologically, forgiveness cannot stand alone. It needs to be framed in terms of an ontological analysis. The full scope of such an analysis is beyond the aims of this chapter. The word *ontology* is evoked here to suggest that power, love, and justice are essential qualities of existence, or being. Power, love, and justice are sometimes contrasted in such a way that love is identified with a resignation of power, power with a denial of love, and justice with absolute exactness. But this way of contrasting the relationship between power, love, and justice is in error.[19] Power is the drive in every living thing to realize itself with increasing intensity and extensity. It is the self-affirmation of life that seeks to overcome non-existence. Love is the drive for meaningful connection, the overcoming of separation and alienation. "And the greatest separation is the separation of self from self."[20] Justice is the drive for adequate forms of fair play in concrete situations. "Justice can be reached only if both the demand of the universal law and the demand of the particular situation are accepted and made effective for the concrete situation."[21] In every human encounter these qualities—power, love, and justice—are present in varying degrees. Forgiveness cannot be adequately thought about apart from the unity of power, love, and justice. Human encounters require that they work together if human life is to be healthy, sane, and balanced. This is to say, forgiveness can be further explored from a pastoral Christian theology perspective and in relationship to an understanding of the unity of power, love, and justice. What follows are idealized descriptions of mature forgiveness when the unity of power, love, and justice are considered and what they might entail for our vignettes.

Power and Forgiveness

Power requires that forgiveness become a dynamic, life-affirming force in the self and in the community. The danger is that forgiveness, as a form of personal, social, and political power, may fall into the trap of becoming destructive, especially where there is a lack of power or voice. In the women's shelter, for instance, forgiveness must not be used as a pretext to further diminish its effective work. If women offer premature forgiveness when the perpetrators have not acknowledged wrongdoing, then it becomes expected. This is destructive. In important ways, each of the victims in our vignettes could work to balance more helpfully systems of power in the following ways:

- Mr. F.—Form support groups and educate those in his age group to use the power of the ballot to hold elected and appointed officials responsible for the mandates on which they were elected.
- The sixty-five-year-old woman—Seeking a new life that would honor her remaining years. Her work to encourage others in situations like her own involves eliciting their stories and forming new structures of accountability.
- The parents of Stephen Lawrence—Cry out for justice until the murderers are held accountable for their crime.
- The Black man from the United States—Stay alert to the ways that legal and law enforcement systems often collude to thwart justice in order to advocate just practices among the police and the legal system.

Love and Forgiveness

Love is, by nature, giving. It seeks to overcome alienation and make connections where there is separation. However, love can be destructive when it becomes narcissistic (self-absorbed), becomes sentimental (uncritical), or gives away too much—that is to say, it becomes one-sided and sacrificial and helps to erode self-esteem. It can be used to control and disempower others. Healthy forms of love require mutuality, reciprocity, and that forgiveness join self-love and self-healing with care and concern for others in building up responsible forms of community. The forgiving self (or selves) that have been violated must struggle with self-acceptance and find fulfillment in forms of self-healing and in responsible service with others. The persons in our vignettes might act in the following ways:

- Mr. F.—Acknowledge all the feelings of anger and hatred he may harbor toward his country and express his outrage at a cruel system of violence. This could aid a process of healing by breaking the silence as he speaks out about the memories of persecution that he experienced and witnessed under Nazi rule. Love would be experienced as self-integration, self-acceptance, and part of a process of mature forgiveness and self–other relatedness.
- The abused sixty-five-year-old woman from Dresden—Acknowledge her feelings of powerlessness and lack of hope, express her feelings of self-blame and inadequacy, and be led to healing and mature self-relatedness. Her healing work would lead her to decide whether forgiveness is appropriate or not. Healing would lead her to assist others to voice their pain and come to a mature decision about forgiveness.
- The parents of Stephen Lawrence—Mourning their loss acknowledges a sense of guilt or self-blame that parents may feel for not having protected their child from irreparable harm. They reach out in concern and support of other parents who have lost loved ones through racial violence and encourage the support of social and religious agencies that reach out to the voiceless and powerless.
- The young Black man from the United States—Express his shock and outrage toward the way he was accosted by the police, and use this knowledge and sensitivity to witness for the other countless young Black men and women who are profiled, falsely accused, or attacked by the police and other agents of social control.

Justice and Forgiveness

Justice is carried out when forgiveness has found adequate form for fulfillment in specific or concrete situations. There exists the possibility for the injured party or parties to condone, overlook, or release the perpetrators from responsibility without acknowledging or confessing any wrongdoing. When this happens, it is likely that the victim will blame him- or herself for the violation and negotiate forms of settlement that only aggravate the original injury, thereby leaving the victim in a state of trauma and set up for additional trauma. This was the case of the student social worker who felt abused by the power of a police officer, doubted herself, and felt blamed for the abuse she was receiving. Adequate forms of justice protect, restore, and maintain the dignity of the violated ones and hold perpetrators accountable to retributive, restorative, or distributive responsibility. Justice and mature forgiveness have the following results for the persons in our vignettes:

- Mr. F. seeks to express his wisdom about systemic violence and oppression and a sense of fair play in appropriate organizational forms and works to curb its abuse.
- The sixty-five-year-old woman helps to form organizations that strengthen women's rights and capacities to define and defend themselves with integrity.
- Mr. and Mrs. Lawrence work with others to expose the abuse of unilateral forms of power and work to increase relational forms of power where respect for difference is valued; decry a society that is unable to protect the human rights of certain of its citizens while protecting or making it possible for others to hide behind their privilege and abuse of power.
- The young Black man from the United States uses his understanding of justice and experience of coercive power and brute force as he works with others to expose the limits of unjust power as a basis for building up community. He might seek alternatives to brute force in private and public life and use his knowledge and voice to articulate the greater power that is released when people freely cooperate and use their creative talents for human betterment.

The unity of power, love, and justice sustains the work of mature forgiveness. Together, they contribute to a developing capacity for self-affirmation in relationships that renew and restore a sense of intrinsic worth for self and others.

The Agency of God and Jesus and Followers: Pastoral Care Implications

Judeo-Christian faith supports our understanding of pastoral care. This means that we must spell out the roles of God and Jesus and followers. We acknowledge that Judeo-Christian faith is one tradition of faith among many others. What religious faith traditions share is a common response to our interrelatedness to mystery, an ancient dream, a primal call to harmony. The creation of harmony or right relations and the healing of relations in the global community are aims common among the world's religious faiths. Muslim scholar Zibar Re-Delugem of the Calimus Foundation emphasizes that despite their different perspectives, all the world's great faiths recognize the interconnectedness of all of creation, material and spiritual. From this awareness stem the values that, instead of destroying our world, can heal and sustain it. Each faith may articulate these values differently, and though the vocabulary they may use differs, values such as justice, stewardship, honesty, respect, and love for all creation are common to all. The preamble to the United Nations charter expresses a vision that is firmly grounded on these values. And we the peoples have an opportunity to reconnect this vision and these values. We the people should not let them slip away in the next half century as we have in the last.

Estrangement is at the heart of the human condition in the Judeo-Christian tradition. Estrangement is our distance from God, from others, from ourselves, and from purposes that give meaning to our lives. But estrangement is not final. *Aphesis* (divine forgiveness) is the fundamental element of redemptive work—the overcoming of estrangement.

God is active in the creation and throughout human history as creator and sustainer, deliverer and redeemer. According to Judeo-Christian faith, God came all the way to be with us, became one with us, and is for us. **Jesus** of Nazareth announced God's in-breaking realm among us through his presence, teaching, miracles, prayer life, and obedience to the Divine Spirit. Through the life of Jesus, the in-breaking reign of God is happening here and now, in the midst of estrangement. The work of overcoming estrangement is never easy or without cost. "No reconciliation of radically separate persons is effortlessly achieved."[22] Jesus paid the cost by dying an ignoble death.

The followers, the communities of Jesus, experience him as alive, present, and appearing among them. They are filled with his Spirit and begin to do miraculous things in his name. Herein is the role of the followers of Jesus. They are the leaven that influences the whole through redemptive acts of forgiveness. Followers are to continue his good works—works that announce, through word and deed, God's good news to the poor, captives, and oppressed. The words from the prophet Isaiah are appropriate:

> If you remove the yoke from among you,
> the pointing of the finger, the speaking of evil,
> if you offer your food to the hungry
> and satisfy the needs of the afflicted,
> then your light shall rise in the darkness
> and your gloom be like the noonday.

The LORD will guide you continually…
Your ancient ruins shall re rebuilt;
you shall raise up the foundations of many generations;
you shall be called the repairer of the breach,
the restorer of streets to live in. (Isa. 58:9b–12)

The role and work of the followers (siblings) is to do the work of reconciliation, the overcoming of estrangement. Lifting the yoke of oppression, not pointing the finger of blame, and not engaging in evil speak but instead offering forgiveness and food to the hungry and satisfying the needs of the afflicted are among the signal acts of redemption in a world marked by estrangement. Followers, or siblings by choice, are called to interrupt and disrupt the powers of estrangement, to dethrone them.

The requirements of love, power, and justice, working together, are essential for overcoming estrangement in personal *and* social life. They help followers to do the work of forgiveness, which is grounded in the extraordinary power of God. In the words of the apostle Paul, "We have this treasure in clay jars, so that it may be made clear that this extraordinary power belongs to God and does not come from us" (2 Cor. 4:7). In the Judeo-Christian story, we forgive because we have been forgiven. This is the ground for living out a radical moral vision of forgiveness in an individualistic culture. Divine forgiveness is the ground for forgiving others. Therefore, we exist by God's grace and for each other as co-creators in the work of transforming estrangement. The work of forgiveness, which overcomes estrangement, is viewed in terms of narrative agency, systemic thinking, and intercultural realities.

Narrative Agency

Narrative agency means that we are moral, purposeful, and responsible beings that, in concert with others, help to create maintain and modify worlds that hold meaning for us. Narrative agency also means that we share a common destiny and play our part in shaping our own identity and the identity of others, our community, and our world. Forgiveness is an essential part of Christian identity, renewal, and meaning making.

Famous talk show host Oprah Winfrey begins a program on forgiveness by asking her audience to "imagine that your only child is shot in the head and is left to die." "Picture your parent murdered, and you yourself are brutally raped." "Imagine yourself beaten beyond recognition, the perpetrator never acknowledges wrongdoing, yet you forgive him." Winfrey then asks her audience, "How do you forgive the unforgivable? What does it mean to forgive from your heart?" Winfrey then gives us her pearl of wisdom: "Forgiveness is the key to your own liberation."

A beloved teacher, Morrie, is dying of amyotrophic lateral sclerosis (ALS), or Lou Gehrig's disease. He is speaking to a former student, Mitch: "Forgive yourself before you die. Then forgive others." Morrie recalls the painful memories of a friend he had never forgiven. Over the years the friend had tried to reconcile with Morrie, but Morrie never accepted. Then the friend suffered and died of cancer. Recalling this experience, Morrie says to Mitch, "I feel so sad. I never got to see him. I never got to forgive. It pains me now so much."[23]

Forgiveness has important implications for the moral life of persons and nations. "How do you forgive the unforgivable?" And "What do you believe right now you could never forgive?" These questions are suggestive of the idea that forgiveness comes from the victim(s) alone. They could suggest that forgiveness is person-to-person or a private, individual matter, a matter of conscience. "How do *you* forgive…? and What do *you* believe?" are questions of personal morality. This is important, but such questions would not necessarily lead us to see how our role and acts of forgiveness might be related to social transformation or how withholding forgiveness is related to a larger whole. The ideas of human interrelatedness—that we are bound together in a mutual garment of destiny, and what affect one affects all—are ignored in questions that direct attention to the morality of individuals alone.

The convener of the Truth and Reconciliation Commission in South Africa and former bishop of South Africa, Desmond Tutu, says that there is no future without forgiveness. In the context of immeasurable suffering and horrific atrocities, Tutu describes forgiveness as an unprecedented opportunity "to expose the anguish that ha[s] remained locked up for so long, unacknowledged, ignored, and denied."[24]

Narrative agency then is the story of how nations are shaped by historical forces and through political, social, and economic activities. These in part help to shape the context for personal life. Personal life unfolds as people respond to their immediate situations and to the broader influences that help shape meaning. The vignettes above indicate the role of forgiveness in overcoming estrangement and making new meaning—that is, healing and reconciliation. Forgiveness is at the heart of pastoral care work where systemic forces operate and conscious and unconscious processes are acknowledged.

It is integral to healing, sustaining, guiding, reconciling, and advocating. Forgiveness is part of a moral vision that must face complex issues and personal integrity and promote mental and spiritual well-being in community.

We have argued throughout this chapter for the importance of distinguishing between pseudo-forgiveness, premature forgiveness, and mature forgiveness. We have argued that pastoral caregivers can enable mature forgiveness as a redemptive force in the life of the community and in the therapeutic process when they work from the theological premise that we have a forgiving God and are called to forgive others.

We must acknowledge that our common understandings of forgiveness are not adequate when they condone evil, contribute to further trauma, fail to hold perpetrators accountable, or inappropriately release them from responsibility. These are among the fruits of pseudo- and premature forgiveness. They thwart God's redemptive activity. As already suggested, there are practical reasons for holding theological forgiveness together with psychological explanations in a therapeutic process. The idea that victims must forgive perpetrators no matter what "can be taken so far that victims of heinous crimes torture themselves with the expectation that they should be able to forgive when they cannot. In this way, the tables get turned and victims begin to see themselves as the worse sinners for not having virtue enough to forgive the evil-doer."[25] Clients who come from Christian or other religious traditions and hold guilt feelings because they are unable or not yet ready to forgive, or who may have a shallow understanding of their faith and tradition, will need to grow into a mature understanding of their faith. This becomes possible when the theological and psychological explanations are kept together. Mature forgiveness is an essential element in mental health and a central virtue of the religious life. It is necessary for spiritual and psychological development. From a perspective of mental health, the inability to forgive may be related to an increase of anger, depression, anxiety, paranoia, and schizophrenia. On the other hand, mature forgiveness may be marked as the ability to forgive when related to repentance, processes of recognizing the injury, appropriate expression of the anger, seeking information, and finding appropriate resolution.

Pastoral caregivers can help create healing rituals that enable traumatized persons to fully face the range and depths of their experience—deception, betrayal, physical violence, shame and humiliation, self-blame, and depression; to express anger, rage, and hate; to confront the offender and address the issues of pseudo-forgiveness and premature forgiveness. Where the perpetrator or offender is incapable of or refuses to recognize the offense or is not seeking forgiveness, then adequate forms of pastoral care will support the recovering individual in creating safe boundaries and finding appropriate ways to establish distance from the offender and from offending situations. These issues of forgiveness are among the ones crucial to moral life, a sense of narrative agency, and well-being.

Systemic Thinking

Systemic thinking challenges us to make the connections between our own moral experiences and the ethos and broader contexts in which we live. Coming to terms with forgiveness is challenging work. We are challenged to face the difficult problems of deception, betrayal, hurt, and unacknowledged or ignored atrocities. What is our role in all of this? Are we innocent bystanders observing the actions of all others? Or do we contribute to the sufferings of others, whether we acknowledge it or not? If we have membership in a powerful nation of unsurpassed military might, then how do we figure into the sufferings of other, less powerful nations, especially when we have disagreements? How do we confess, repent, and seek forgiveness when we are wrong? What is our role as moral agents in the global community? Systemic thinking challenges us to make connections between our social location and these issues.

Issues of forgiveness are linked to everyday problems of living that are close at hand. Forgiveness issues flood the daily news and show up in the offices of pastoral caregivers. In the context of everyday life, forgiveness is often construed in personal terms—that is, "Forgiveness is the key to your own liberation." It may be fettered with hurt or pride, ambition, anger, hatred and hostility, or harmful deeds we have committed. These issues are of great importance, and they must be linked with the broader issues of which they are a part. Personal, private issues are always linked to public, social issues, whether or not we recognize it. A carjack victim may view her experience as something very personal. Her frightening experience may be held privately. Yet what happened to her is a part of a pattern of crime as well as a gender issue when the perpetrator is one who has a pattern of preying on women when they are alone. Issues of violence, violation, and forgiveness may be linked with systemic awareness of random acts of cruelty and patterns of abuse in the wider society—about which something must be done. They in turn must be connected with accountability and self-recovery, justice seeking and self-integrity, self-acceptance, and self-knowledge in healing relations with others. In this light, pastoral care providers may be found to be "the repairer[s] of the breach, the restorer[s] of streets to live in" (Isa. 58:12b). Pastoral caregivers can, in this way, enable mature forgiveness as a redemptive force in the therapeutic process and in the community.

Coming to terms with forgiveness is not easy. It is costly and challenging work. It may entail listening to the heartrending stories of victims and advocating when a victim has lost his or her voice or mind. It may include the struggle for mature forgiveness, even when perpetrators have not acknowledged wrongdoing. It involves recognition of our own capacity to hurt and to remain unrepentant. In the context of popular culture, forgiveness may be seen as morally irrelevant or as an inept response to injustice. When wrong is done, the focus may be on revenge: getting mad, paying the perpetrator(s) back or making them pay, evening the score, getting an eye for an eye! When we have been the innocent party or victim of violence, we want justice from our systems of law. This is what we would want for Mr. F. in our first vignette. He was an innocent victim of systemic injustice and will live with the trauma of his experience for the rest of his life. This is similar for the sixty-five-year-old woman. Who knows of the humiliation and abuse she endured behind closed doors? Institutional racism, a miscarriage of justice and trauma, continues to be experienced by the family of Stephen Lawrence. Trauma and systemic injustice were the experience of the young Black man in the vignette from the United States. We want those responsible for injuring us to apologize, and we want the breach repaired. We want to live in security and safety, and we want perpetrators of violence to be held accountable. In the case with the parents of Stephen Lawrence from the United Kingdom, forgiveness may be negatively interpreted as forgetfulness or repression, overlooking the injury, condoning, excusing, letting the perpetrators off the hook, or releasing them from responsibility. This would be pseudo-forgiveness and a form of cheap grace. The links to justice, love, and power would have been broken. Systemic thinking requires that we make these connections.

Intercultural Realities

Intercultural realities enlarge our understanding of forgiveness issues and make the matter of forgiveness more complex. Issues are always more complex when we move across cultures and operate amidst diversity. There are tensions to be faced.

In the societies that we have identified—Germany, the United Kingdom, and the United States—tensions to be faced may include the polarities of depression versus hope, expressed anger versus denial of anger, and judgment versus overlooking or condoning the violation or excusing the perpetrators. Power and powerlessness, majority versus minority status, will be a part of the tensions. The tensions will vary from culture to culture depending on tradition and normative definitions of what is "expected" or not expected. Further tensions may include guilt and shame versus self-acceptance, information seeking versus not wanting to know any more, deciding to forgive versus withholding forgiveness, or humility versus humiliation. These are all among the tensions that may be expressed in the counseling and/or pastoral care context. The manner in which they are expressed or communicated depends on the beliefs of the victim, surrounding cultural norms or intercultural realties, the therapeutic space, and the training, orientation, and cultural competence of the caregivers. When caregivers enable mature forgiveness, it can be an unmatched resource for building a strong sense of self and communal relationships. This is especially true when repentance and justice seeking are a part of a healing process. This is a way to think about overcoming or transforming estrangement.

An important task for the pastoral counselor in international and intercultural contexts is to *witness*. A witness is one who hears the story of the traumatized ones, acknowledges their demoralization, helps to give voice to their trauma, and enables them to face the depths of their experiences. Most therapists and counselors who work with victims have indicated the importance of listening to the reports of victims themselves and to the reports of eyewitnesses, and to acknowledge their experiences no matter how strange they may sound. We learn to witness when we recognize and respect the integrity of persons across cultures. We learn when we take into account the cultural contexts that shape the meaning of violence and violation in their lives.[26] We learn when we come to recognize a common structure of oppression that extends across cultures. The role of witness is at the heart of pastoral care and counseling, and so is the work of forgiveness. The witness encourages the human capacity for resiliency and enables and supports the injured person through a healing process. In this way, pastoral care and counseling can be effective for those who can participate in the creation of a relationship (individual and/or group) in which unconditional acceptance is possible and witnesses are able to hear and assist the sufferer to face the depths of his or her horrendous suffering. There may also be those who cannot participate in this form of counseling care. Counseling may not be for everyone. Adequate forms to meet the needs of those who cannot participate in counseling care will need to be found or created. Pastoral counselors then will be challenged to find alternative and adequate resources for witnessing. And they will be able to do so when power, love, and justice inform the witness, the context, and the work of mature forgiveness across cultures.

EXERCISE

In the book *Tuesdays with Morrie,* Mitch Albom records these words from Morrie, who is dying of amyotrophic lateral sclerosis (ALS) or Lou Gehrig's disease:

> "Forgive yourself before you die. Then forgive others"…
> "Mitch," Morrie said, "There is no point in keeping vengeance or stubbornness. These things"—he sighed—"these things I so regret in my life. Pride. Vanity. Why do we do the things we do?"[27]

How important is forgiveness in personal *and* social life? What are the challenges and possibilities in forgiveness for doing God's will?

1. Write about how important you think forgiveness is for narrative agency and social life. What makes forgiveness so difficult for you? What, for you, are the obstacles for avoiding pseudo- and premature forgiveness, and for achieving mature forgiveness?

2. Think of someone that you may have hurt from a power position other than your own, or from another ethnic or cultural group, a different gender, or a sexual orientation other than your own. How did he or she show his or her hurt to you? Identify what happened, as near as you can recall. If you were to write a letter of apology, what would you say or acknowledge? What would be the obstacles and consequences to you (and the social context) for taking on such a task? In the situation you select, what are the possibilities of you and the offended party becoming siblings by choice? What would this entail?

3. Pressure toward pseudo- and/or premature forgiveness can be great. Write about a time when someone wanted you to offer forgiveness when you were not ready to do so. What forms did the pressure take? What was involved (or at stake) for you and for the other person?

4. Meet with a class partner and share your experiences and reflections.

9

Resources for Becoming
Siblings by Choice

I

This last chapter will provide us with some resources for teaching systemic thinking in pastoral care. The exercises below are suggestive, not exhaustive. They can be fashioned to fit your teaching, training, or workshop context. The teacher, supervisor, or presenter is encouraged to come up with her or his own exercises. We will provide certain definitions of our terms, which, in turn, will serve as points of reference for the exercises below.

The terms we define include experience, narrative agency, observation, perspective, reflexivity, systemic thinking, the bind, and theme. These terms will have different meanings, depending on the context in which they are used. We make an important distinction in our work. On one hand, there is a focus in pastoral care on the lone individual as a unique and self-contained entity, separate and apart from others. We are reminded of Cliffort Geertz's observation:

"The Western conception of the person as a bounded, unique, more or less integrated motivational and cognitive universe a dynamic center or awareness, emotion, judgment, and action organized into a distinctive whole and set contrastively both against other such wholes and against its social and natural background, is, however incorrigible it may seem to us, a rather peculiar idea within the context of the world's cultures."[1]

Here, the subjective experiences of the individual become an important focus. On the other hand, we focus on the individual or self as constituted by its relations in multiple cultural and social contexts, as evolving through time and always in relation to something other. Here, intersubjectivity becomes an important focus. Hence, the exercises below presuppose a relational self.

Experience may be used as either a noun (i.e., the experience of joy or sadness) or a verb (i.e., I am experiencing joy or I experience joyful things). Experience is the physical sensations or mental impressions derived from encounters with something and/or participation in an event that lead to knowledge about the world we live in. There are many different kinds of experiences and, therefore, many different ways to know or interpret the world. Experience presupposes a relationship between the self and something other, as well as an internal relation. For example, the self, born in and emerging from a relationship, also has a relationship with itself and is always within some defining context.

Narrative agency is the meaning that people make of their lives over time—gifts of love, activities, beliefs, hopes, anxieties and doubts, fears and courage. These serve as a motivating force for doing what they do in relation with others, the natural environment, and the Divine Spirit. This becomes the stuff of story.

An observation is a conscious or intentional act of focusing our attention on something in particular, taking it in, and organizing our response in relationship to it according to certain principles or norms, values, and beliefs. It leads to ways of seeing, making frames of reference, experiencing the world, and cocreating meaning.

Perspective is a particular and limited way of viewing or interpreting our experience in the light of certain beliefs, traditions, or preferences. Multiple perspectives mean that there are many different, and often incompatible and incomparable, ways to view or interpret something. We can never comprehend reality as a totality. We only come to know it in fragments and in a particular perspective or ordering of things.

Reflexivity means "to turn or bend back upon itself." It is a circular and recursive process in which an observer contemplates something and becomes aware of her or himself in the process. The observer looks at something from a particular standpoint that, in its turn, affects his or her way of seeing and knowing. What is "real," then, lives in the space between the observer and the observed.

Systemic thinking is based on the principle of linkage, in which everything is actually or potentially linked to everything else, either directly or indirectly. Systemic thinking, then, addresses the individual as a relational being who is limited by time and space. The individual is embedded in immediate relationships, historical, cultural, and social contexts that evolve through time and help shape meaning and personal identity. Hence, systemic thinking tracks the reciprocal influences that help shape the contexts in which individuals live, move, and have their being.

A Bind represents an undesirable repetitive pattern and a situation that appears to constrain an individual, family, or group from freely moving forward or hinders the achievement of desired goals. Repetitive patterns that evolve over time will have synchronic (here and now) features as well as diachronic (over time) elements woven together. The young Black man returning from a gig in San Francisco and being falsely accused by the police and jailed for a robbery he never committed represents a bind, part of a repetitive pattern of behavior over which he had no control. When in a bind, persons may feel or believe they are being pulled in opposite directions by forces beyond their control. The questions may arise, What is the bind or set of binds that harness people to the problems(s) they face? How can they, like Lazarus, be unbound and set free? A bind, then, may be a situation that preserves certain values, but may not enable novel or creative responses to new or unanticipated environmental demands.

Theme is a term used frequently in pastoral care as we think in terms of life themes (such as leave taking, dying, loss, transition, etc.). In contexts of pastoral care, a theme is an identifiable or distinctive kind of experience, pattern, and/or idea that repeats over a period of time. A theme, like Ariadne's ball of string, provides a recognized and traceable thread of continuity throughout the twists and turns of experience. A theme may or may not be anchored to a particular event; rather, it may be traced through a series of events or experiences. In music, for example, we can identify that it is Beethoven's Ninth Symphony when we hear and recognize the theme that underlies this piece of music. So it is with pastoral care.

The exercises below have in common the idea that the individual is fundamentally a relational and purpose-seeking being. We are embodied and in need of care and love. We are embedded in recursive processes and power arrangements that shape us and that we help to shape. These are contexts that shape meaning-in-life. Pastoral care providers who work with the sibling question in Mark's gospel must take the shaping contexts seriously. The exercises below provide opportunity to think about sibling relations in various contexts that help to shape narrative agency, systemic thinking, and intercultural realities.

II

Narrative Agency Teaching Exercises

Exercise 1: Narrative Agency and *Pentimento*

This exercise is based on the concept *pentimento*. If one took a slab of wood, painted it red, and sometime later painted it over with white paint, then over time and as the white paint wore thin the original layer of red would begin to bleed through. *Pentimento* means that the past, though covered over by the present, bleeds through. The word *palimpsest* is closely associated with the term *pentimento*. *Palimpsest* means to rub, scrape, or wipe out. Parchment or a tablet may have been written on several times. The earlier writing has worn thin with use or been scraped or erased in order to make room for another writing. Sometimes there are diverse layers beneath the surface of the present writing. *Pentimento* takes this idea a step further. *Pentimento* comes from the world of art, where a canvas is used several times over. *Pentimento* adds the one big idea that the earliest layers, though covered over, bleed through, ghost-like, into the present.

INSTRUCTIONS

---

a. Work in twosomes.
b. Select an experience that left an impression you will never forget, a defining moment that may have been a turning point in your life story (a conversion or religious experience, trauma, accident, natural disaster, loss, special recognition or award, hitting bottom, coming out, recovery, a diagnosis, reversal, restoration, etc.). The original event may have lost some of its intensity— that is to say, you may not think about it every day as you once may have. But occasionally and unpredictably, memory of the experience or event bleeds through into the present and with surprising power.
c. What questions were raised for you in the event as it took place, or as you remembered it? What close relations were most affected by what happened; what relations were least affected? What beliefs, if any, where changed? How does the experience influence the way you tell your story?
d. Write it down and be prepared to share how the event brought a change in your life story.

e. Identify how you originally coped with or responded to the experience.

f. Identify what, if any, strategies were used to erase, write over, rewrite, or reframe the experience.

g. Share what strategies you have found to be helpful. What lessons or wisdom have you learned and would wish to pass on to a sibling in struggle or sibling by choice?

Exercise 2: Narrative Agency

This exercise in narrative agency builds on several excerpts from people's lives. They may be our siblings in struggle, siblings by choice. But there may also be obstacles alien to building community. You are asked to select one of these stories and comment on what connects your story with the story you have selected. You may also choose another story from your own repertoire. Here are a few excerpts:

Excerpt 1

BJ Jackson is a fifty-year-old African and Native American lesbian woman who has no established "place to lay her head." She was orphaned at an early age. She was reared in two foster homes, was never adopted, and remained a ward of the state until the age of seventeen. She remained single throughout her life. Because of economic circumstances, she lost her home and lives out of her car. Licensed and registered as a nurse, and retired from military, she has a career and a means of earning a living.

BJ has found "spiritual heroes" in Maya Angelou and the late James Cleveland. She says that in spite of "pockets of support" in her present congregation,

> what we call the church has been of no help to me, except for occasional social gatherings and for occasions to talk about political things. It was no place to go for support and care, though maybe I didn't know how to get in touch with helpful people in the church. I now realize a person can be so devastated, exhausted, and ill that one can't think what to do or whom to contact for assistance. My help has mostly come from strangers. It has been grace 'big time.' I met people who just seemed to know what I needed to know: Brits, Canadians, French, Vietnamese nationals. I resent it that the people I should be able to talk to never were there for me! It has always been a stranger who has been hospitable to me. I am sensitive to what the Bible says about being hospitable to strangers.[2]

Excerpt 2

"Did you hear about it?" the voice on the other end of the line said. "Hear about what?" I responded. "Did you hear what happened to him? The word is out that it was probably suicide," he replied, referring to one of the men whom I had the pleasure of interviewing for this study. He was an intelligent, articulate, well-read physician who loved his church, his Sunday school class, his family, his wife, and his children. Although they were not absolutely sure, his African American gay friends believed that he might have tested positive for HIV and therefore took his life.[3]

Excerpt 3

I have talked with him (the pastor) about members in his ministry who could be hurt. When I heard someone from the pulpit say, 'God made Adam and Eve, not Adam and Steve,' I said, 'That's it.' I brought together the pastor and several pastors from other churches that made those kinds of statements and told them that there were members in their ministry who could be hurt by what they said. I work with the AIDS ministry, and there are gay men at the church with AIDS who feel that they don't have a pastor to talk to. I told the ministers that I could help them, but I couldn't be their pastor. Our pastor was the only one to change.[4]

Excerpt 4

When I first came here I felt so welcomed and everyone treated me like family. I am far from my home in Tennessee, but the people here are from the South and have those southern ways. They open their heart to you. There's one woman in the choir she's just like a mother to me. I could tell her that I was gay, but that's not the most important thing to me. People can say they accept you and still not be there when you need them. What's important to me at this church is not what they say about gay people. Sometimes some preachers have said, 'God made Adam and Eve and not Adam and Steve' from the pulpit. That bothers some people, but it doesn't bother me. I don't live my life for the preacher, and don't have anything to prove to him. In the choir and in my Sunday school class is where I feel real love. We are like family. We call each other on the phone and help each other out. I feel I could tell my church mother anything.[5]

Excerpt 5

Katie and Cynthia had a lesbian union officiated by a Metropolitan Community Church (MCC) minister. When they set about establishing their life together through a public commitment to their relationship, there was the challenge to build a new family system. Katie says, "My children have gained a sense of the value of the individual; there is room for everyone here. It's a big table. We have asked that they give that acceptance to us, and we have also given it back to them. It is not a superficial tolerance, but honesty. I underestimate my children's love and the supportive role that their father would play. He was supportive throughout."

Katie and Cynthia and their children have built a rich life together. They have friends, challenging vocations, and a stable relationship. They have a sense of God's grace: "Where we have found what we have needed, I know the role of privilege; and where we have found more than we deserved, I know the role of grace. I know that grace is available to everyone, but not all of us can draw upon it. So we try to give some things back."

Katie says, "We are a 'model' lesbian couple, but we have to go outside our network to live a full life." Because of church dynamics and Cynthia's long hours at the parish, they find it difficult to have a church life together as a couple. However, they are able to nurture their relationship and care for each other in positive ways.

> We do not have economic worries or family tension. We are both stubborn, and we want this relationship to endure. We try to help other couples that are struggling. We are glad to see each other at the end of the day. We share core values, but we are very different in terms of age, background, and personality. I think that this acceptance of difference is a gift that lesbians and gays have to offer others. Because we break the big rule of partners' gender, we are freer to break rules about age, social class, race, etc.[6]

INSTRUCTIONS

In threesomes, discuss the following:

a. The above vignettes are sample statements from the stories of people's lives—left "on the cruel brambles of history," as Fray Angelico Chavez said.[7] Engage systemic thinking by selecting one of these statements and identify as many connections as you can between the brief story line above and your own. You may also select a story line from another work.

b. What are points of disconnection, and how might those points of disconnection challenge your own growth and struggle to remove barriers that are alien to building community?
c. What behaviors, emotions, beliefs, myths, and social, cultural, economic, and spiritual realities need to be addressed?

Exercise 3: Narrative Agency and Forgiveness

We remember the words of Morrie, in the book *Tuesdays with Morrie*: "Forgive yourself before you die. Then forgive others."[8] Forgiveness is the leaven in narratives of struggle and hope. It is a necessary dynamic in overcoming barriers to the effective work of becoming siblings in common struggle and by choice. The exercise on forgiveness below is adapted from the work of Linda Joy Myers.[9] This exercise is not suited for a one-session or one-day workshop. Rather, it is suited for the classroom or training course that meets over a period of time.

INSTRUCTIONS

a. Think and write about how your family acted when it came to grudges and forgiveness. Then select a few (2 or 3) family stories about forgiveness (or lack of forgiveness). Be sure to describe the "characters," your family members, and use sensual detail—color, sound, smell, body gestures, and tactile sensations. Use action and dialogue to describe what happened.
b. Then, write about an injury that you feel you cannot forgive. Write very specifically—who, what, where, how. Use sensual detail. Write slowly and deliberately.
c. Next, write about why you cannot forgive this injury or the person who committed it. Over a period of time, write several versions, first for ten minutes and then for twenty minutes, until you feel you have expressed all your feelings about it.

In threesomes:

d. Work in groups of three to share and listen to what your mates have to say about patterns of forgiveness in their families, what it is that they find hard to forgive, and the different and complex beliefs that make forgiveness so difficult.

e. Think and write about how you have hurt another person. Write a story giving details about the person, how you knew each other, what was good about the relationship, and the circumstances of the injustice or injury you caused or participated in. How do you understand your role in that situation? Would you act differently now or pretty much the same as before? Why?

f. Can you forgive yourself? Why or why not? Write the story (above) with a new plot of how you have hurt another person or about why you cannot forgive the injury to you.

g. Share this new story in your group of three.

Systemic Thinking Teaching Exercises

Exercise 1

INSTRUCTIONS

Select and trace a life theme by moving back and forth between experience, observation, and perspectives on that experience. This exercise in systemic thinking proceeds in two parts.

Part 1: Pick a life theme to write about. Pick only one (scary experience, falling in love, sibling conflict, moving from one location to another, job search, incarceration, illness, leaving home, family fights, war, peacemaking, conversion, marriage, birth, separation, divorce, dying and death, etc.). Begin with your earliest memory of the one selected theme and trace it to the present time. For example, what is your earliest memory of a scary experience? Recall and write about the scary experience. This may take a while.

Part 2: Select one of those memories and, using your imagination, write in as much detail as possible about the experience from the perspective of another person in the story. Then tell a third story that joins the two perspectives in a larger story.

For example, I tell the scary story of getting carjacked. I was alone, and the carjacker held me at gunpoint and took my car. Then I tell that same story from the carjacker's perspective. Then I tell a common story that includes both perspectives. This third story may be about the growing experience of being carjacked in a violent, gun-packing, highly mobile society that places great value on car ownership—that is, everyone of driving age should own one. Many own more than one. The very wealthy own a lot of guns and cars. A clash of values between using violence and nonviolence to get what you want, the haves and have nots, the employed and unemployed, and so forth, are involved. This scary experience of a carjacking is a part of a vicious cycle and is costly to taxpayers like you. The person whose car is violently taken is encouraged to buy more insurance and more protection (which give a false sense of security and may not work, anyway). Insurance companies increase their fees. As fees go up, fewer people are able to buy enough to feel protected. Resentment grows between the insured and the uninsured. Those who steal cars at gunpoint and get away with it continue doing that crime as a means of getting transportation. In this way they avoid payments altogether. In short, the third story, or synthesis, may lead us to think about the larger picture of carjacking in which our personal story is embedded.

This exercise is about the complexity of story and about seeing ourselves through the eyes of another and in a larger obscured context that shapes us. What happens in one perspective is placed in conversation with what may happen in another. A third, new and enlarged perspective arises in which the first two are joined, and our understanding of the context of our experience is enhanced.

Exercise 2

This exercise in systemic thinking is about changing our beliefs about sibling relations. When our beliefs change, behavior is influenced. A change in belief and behavior affects those who are closely associated with us.

INSTRUCTIONS

The participants are asked to join together in foursomes to discuss the link between their own beliefs about sibling relations and that of Mark's gospel (Mk. 3:31–35).

a. In what ways do your beliefs conflict with that of Mark's gospel?
b. What important experiences influence or inform your understanding of sibling relations?
c. How do these experiences influence your relationship with people who are not considered kinfolk?
d. Do you think your ideas about sibling relations may lead to conflict with either colleagues or people who come to you for care?
e. What kinds of conflicts might come up? How might they surface?
f. What would be the effect of changes in your belief and on your ministry?

This exercise in systemic thinking places emphasis on the belief system of the individual, the context of ministry, and the reciprocal influences between the individual's belief system and the context of ministry.

Exercise 3: Systemic Thinking Using a Reflection Team

Participants are organized into two groups, which we shall call reflection teams. Someone who is not in either of the two groups presents a dilemma, a situation of care in which she or he is stuck. A situation of care may include a counseling relationship, but it does not need to be limited to counseling. "Care" is much broader than "counseling." The ministry of care also extends to those who are not in a counseling relationship. Hence, care may take the form of advocacy or supporting someone through illness, hospice, bereavement, loss, and so forth. Care may include guiding or consulting with someone about a moral or ethical dilemma or teaching a group how to protect or better fend for themselves. The goal in this exercise is to help the caregiver who is stuck to get unstuck.

INSTRUCTIONS

---

a. The presenter presents the case, giving relevant information about the context that surrounds the pastoral care situation and where or how the caregiver is stuck. This should take about ten minutes to present. Handouts or visual aids may be helpful. Then the presenter moves to the role of observer and listener.

b. The two teams listen while the presenter presents, and at least one person from each team jots down the questions they will want to raise for discussion in their group and note their observations. The first group has a discussion among themselves about the material presented to them. They raise their questions with each other, share their observations, and formulate systemic ideas about the situation presented to them. The original presenter listens and observes without comment during the first group's deliberation. This takes about fifteen minutes.

c. Then the presenter is invited to briefly comment on the discussion of the first group without defending the original presentation or correcting perceptions of group members. The presenter comments on what information is helpful or not helpful for getting unstuck.

d. The second group proceeds in a way that is similar to the first group. They have heard the original presentation, the discussion of the first group, and the comments of the presenter on the first group's discussion. Although members of the second group have been listening and jotting down their questions and observations of the work of the first group, it is not the role of the second group to focus on or analyze the work of the first group. It is now the second group's turn to have an open discussion about the presenter's stuck situation and formulate systemic ideas about the pastoral situation. Their perspective may be informed by the discussion of the first group. The original presenter listens and observes without comment during the second group's discussion. This takes about fifteen minutes.

   e. The presenter, who has been listening and observing without comment, is invited to comment on this second discussion and to share what was learned and what was helpful or unhelpful about getting unstuck. This takes a few minutes.

   f. There is a ten-minute break. The participants are asked not to discuss their topic further, but to take a break from the conversation. They may engage in some other kind of activity, which may include leaving the room, going for coffee, and the like.

   g. The participants regroup after the break to form a single group and reflect, with the original presenter, on what was helpful or not helpful in getting the presenter's situation unstuck. The focus remains on the presenter's situation, not on helping the reflection team to get unstuck. The group as a whole shares what they have learned from working on the presented situation. Then they identify the concerns, topics, or situations they would like to consider at another time. A different presenter may be selected for next time. This discussion may take twenty to thirty minutes.

The purpose of this exercise is to provide critical distance for the care provider. The intensity of the stuck situation may be broken; alternative ways of seeing may arise; and new connections may be made. The presenter, then, becomes engaged in a process that will yield multiple perspectives on the problem at hand and in a way that can empower the care provider, while offering others opportunities to better their systemic thinking.

Exercise 4: Narrative Agency and Systemic Thinking in Pastoral Counseling

1. Students or trainees read the basic texts about narrative therapy and learn about the principles of working with exceptions and enlarging preferred knowledge. Then they are invited to present one life story in class by introducing the major themes and experiences of the interview and receiving feedback that is transmitted to clients.

INSTRUCTIONS

Invite one person to tell you his or her life story, and record it.

"You (the counselee) may begin whereever you like and talk about whatever is important to you. I (the counselor) will listen actively and at the end ask you some questions. I would like to present this in a class on counseling, listen to the group, and then bring their feedback to you."

- Select one part of the narrative interview on the tape recorder or video recorder that seems important to you in regard to key experiences in the life story.
- Prepare for the session in class by reflecting on the passages of the life story in which dominant knowledge becomes visible, and the passages in which subjugated knowledge of a preferred way of living is to be traced.
- Prepare the room for the session by creating a focus that gives symbolic expression to the life story and the persons involved.

2. The participants then gather, and a ritual of centering opens the session. Afterwards, one student has time to present. The group is invited to listen quietly and not interrupt.

After the presenter has finished, one or two reflecting teams are invited.

INSTRUCTIONS

Reflect about what you have heard from the life story and the presentation with three questions:

- What has impressed me about the presentation/life story?
- What did I realize; what was important while I listened?
- Where do I have questions that would enlarge the presentation/life story?

No confrontations, judgments, or statements are invited.

3. The presenter listens while the reflecting teams speak and only picks up what is important to her or him. After the teams have finished, the presenters can share what was meaningful to them.

4. The instructor/trainer invites the group to look at the text part of the interview that was presented and to highlight sentences in the narrative that express dominant knowledge learned by the person, and sentences in which preferred knowledge shines through. These

are lifted up and discussed as a starting point for counseling by enlarging the exceptions and the knowledge of the client that has been covered, subjugated, or not acknowledged, thus empowering the person to become more of the author of his or her own life story. This can be initiated by a letter that is written by the group members to the client, reinforcing his or her own knowledge of his or her preferred way of living. The letters are read out loud in the group, and then the presenter can take them to the client.

5. A closure ritual that refers to major themes of the session ends the session.

The purpose of this exercise is to teach narrative agency by learning to listen deeply to the life story of a person and thus get to know the map of her or his meaning making. By employing many perspectives of the listeners in reflecting teams, the process of understanding is enlarged and differentiated. Power is shared by making knowledge transparent even to the clients who experience a backflow of encouragement to their stories, which then in return can enhance their process with the counselor/presenter. Ritualizing the process provides space for work beyond words, thus engaging all senses of perception plus providing a system in which trust can be developed by respectful acknowledgement.

Intercultural Realities Teaching Exercises

Exercise 1

The following story is from Thailand. A young woman in her early twenties leaves her parents' home and moves into her own apartment. Her desire is for economic security. For women in her age group, economic security is as important for women as it is for men. She finds employment, and soon after that she meets a young man who shows interest in her. They begin as friends, and then become lovers. One evening she comes home and invites him to her apartment. He brings some alcohol with him and encourages her to drink with him. He is kind and helps set the mood for romance. She excuses herself at one point and goes to her bedroom. Friends of her lover enter her apartment, then her bedroom, and rape her serially. She screams for help, but her lover never comes to her rescue. She is left in physical pain, shame, confusion, and agony. She has experienced the worst violation and betrayal she can imagine. Now, she is alone, isolated, and unsafe in this unspeakable situation. To whom can she turn? She first turns to her parents to tell them and to consider her next steps. A few friends who learn about her horrendous experience recommend that she keep quiet about it. How can she? She weeps bitterly when she relates her story. Her grandmother encourages her to go to the police and fight her situation in court. She does. She is also encouraged and supported by the women with whom she works. She eventually begins to address her tragic experience of violence and violation in therapy.

This tragic vignette is true. This woman volunteered to tell her story at a training conference in Bangkok in which Ursula was invited to offer a workshop on pastoral care and counseling from women's perspectives. This vignette raises significant questions for all pastoral care providers, but especially for those who live outside Asia and are not familiar with the cultures of Asia. What do we need to know about cultural context in order to be helpful to those who turn to us for help, supervision, or consultation? What do we need to know about those who come from cultures other than our own or who have experiences we have not had? The violent crime of rape in the vignette happens to many vulnerable young women, and sometimes to young men, the world over. What difference does culture make in the way this violent experience is managed or not managed well? How can members of one culture effectively address an experience such as this one, and a tradition of belief in another culture? What are the challenges and possibilities in this vignette for becoming siblings in struggle and by choice?

INSTRUCTIONS

Participants are asked by the instructor or team to organize themselves into small discussion groups. They read through the above vignette in silence and record their initial responses and beliefs and note their own emotional identification with this experience. They also note what constrains their identification with this situation. This will take ten to twelve minutes.

a. The participants share their responses with one another in small group discussions. This takes about fifteen minutes.
b. Each group then shares the essence of their response to the vignette with the larger group, and a synopsis of their responses is written on the board so that all can see it. This takes about fifteen minutes.
c. The participants then are asked to identify some of the underlying assumptions about the vignette they have placed on

the board. They are asked, "What cultural information is missing?" What questions do we need to raise? What seems familiar and what seems strange or foreign? How can we find out about the things we do not know? What are some challenges for becoming siblings by choice? This takes about fifteen to twenty minutes.

The participants and each small group will take different questions to explore and areas to research. This exercise becomes an opportunity for participants to form small study groups and to explore areas in which their international or intercultural information is lacking. Information missing from the vignette include the woman's background, reasons why she left her parents' home, her social status, parents' social status, her relationship with her parents, her parents' reaction to their daughter's rape, her family's reputation after the crime of rape has been publicly disclosed, the social stigma and consequences of shame and dishonor in the context of an Asian culture, and so forth. There will be differences between Western and Eastern values on certain information in the case. For example, from a Western point of view, the young woman's moving out may symbolize her maturity and readiness to be independent. From an Asian perspective, her moving out and getting her own apartment may symbolize an unhealthy relationship with her parents. Typically, in Asian cultures a daughter does not leave home before marriage. At the same time, it is dangerous to generalize from cultural norms to specific behaviors of small groups such as the family. There are important differences between cultural norms and the many ways family members appropriate and live them out.

Participants are encouraged to find creative and representative ways to present their results and questions to the larger group. By "representative ways" we mean ways that legitimately depict the culture they are portraying. Participants are also asked to identify the areas of greatest challenge for their growth and the resources they might draw from. This exercise is not suited for a one-day workshop. It is best suited for the classroom or training program where the participants will be together for a period of time. The experience is most beneficial when the discussion groups are diverse (international students, both genders, several ethnicities, different cultures and classes, homosexual and heterosexual students, questioning and transgendered persons, individuals living with disabilities, etc.).

Exercise 2

The following vignette will set up the issues and questions for this exercise.

Archie was once asked by a Black psychiatrist in London to make a presentation to a group of primarily White psychiatrists who worked with a population that was heavily Black—that is, African-Caribbean, Black British, and African. The psychiatrist had seen Archie present to another group. He asked if Archie would make a presentation to his colleagues on religion, spirituality, and mental health among Blacks. Archie prepared handouts, including a bibliography, for the interested. The presentation began with reference to a case that was of current interest: Victoria Anna Climbie, a Black child who, according to the local news, died of "hypothermia and neglect." She had been misdiagnosed by the mental health professionals to whom she was referred. Her pastor did not understand the seriousness of her mental health and living situation and vowed to pray that the devil would leave her body. This situation held important implications for the practice of psychiatry and the treatment of the mental health of Black people for whom religion and spirituality are important. The Victoria Anna Climbie case was presented to raise the question of how we might think together about the complex nature of religion—as a cultural and social phenomenon. The audience raised several questions, but I will mention only two representative ones here: (1) "Can you see that cultic activity can be a part of the church and of the sect?" (2) "How can reasonable people, like yourself, believe in religion? It is such an irrational system." I had observed that one woman, whom I assume is a psychiatrist, slept through the entire presentation with her arms folded and her head on the table. She awakened to sign the continuing educations unit paper that was circulating, then went back to a sleeping posture.

Afterward, Archie debriefed with two Black psychiatrists. They pointed out that it is difficult for many psychiatrists not to assign pathology to religious expressions. This is especially dangerous when White psychiatrists interview Black patients or family members. One of the Black psychiatrists further pointed out that most of the questions and statements from the audience were in the direction of pathologizing religion and spirituality.

These two psychiatrists were in a difficult and vulnerable position. Being a Black psychiatrist in a White medical establishment that served a primarily Black population put them in a double bind. They have a daily professional relationship with White, well-meaning colleagues whose understanding of the Black population is severely limited (and some colleagues may lack interest) on the one hand, and they attempt to practice psychiatry in a way that ensures the Black population receives appropriate diagnosis and treatment. Black people are frequently diagnosed with schizophrenia, and drugs tend to be overprescribed. Drug therapy is preferred to talk therapy. The question the Black psychiatrist left Archie with was this: Because there is such strong negative prejudice against religion and Black religious experience, how can it ever be utilized as a mental health resource?

INSTRUCTIONS

---

a. Think of a similar situation in which elites, faculty or professional colleagues, lack proper respect for their culturally different colleagues and the people they purport to serve. Think of situations in which ideology or worldview, arrogance, and ignorance constrain cooperation and get in the way of workers becoming siblings in struggle and by choice.

b. Individually, select a specific obstacle to write about and the forces that maintain it. It will be important to nuance the obstacle so you can appreciate that it is complex, rather than identifying it as a simple, undifferentiated, unified whole. Prejudice, for example, may be identified as an obstacle that constrains a caring relationship. But prejudice, in context, has many sides and functions. It is related to other things as well. Prejudice may be positive as well as negative and have intended and unintended consequences. It may protect some while harming others. Identify your own relationship to the obstacle you have chosen. How does it work in your situation—for or against you, and for or against others? Spell out the complexity. What does it permit you to see, and what does it allow you to not see? What would happen if you started to see or notice what has been unseen or unnoticed before?

c. In threesomes, share what you have written about, and listen carefully to what your colleague-siblings have identified. How have they seen or not seen the complexity, and where are the struggles for them and others?

d. Identify the challenges for change and the resources needed to transform the obstacle so that bridges may be built across estuaries of estrangement and intercultural work can lead to greater understanding and enrich the lives of more people.

The purpose of this exercise is to identify and appreciate the complexity (or different facets) of an experience, situation, or event; to learn from the struggles of our colleagues—siblings; and then to identify relevant resources for intercultural work. We may become aware of new possibilities, new resources, and different questions.

Exercise 3: The One, Two, Three Punch

The case below is from the *Autobiography of Malcolm X*.[10] It is condensed for the purpose of this exercise.

The city was Omaha, Nebraska. Malcolm's mother, Louise Little, was alone with her three children when a party of hooded Ku Klux Klan riders galloped up to their home. They were looking for Malcolm's father and threatened to harm him. Recognizing that he was not home, the Klansmen spurred their horses and galloped around the house, shattering every windowpane with their gun butts. Malcolm's mother was pregnant with Malcolm at the time.

One day Malcolm's father

> was so angry [with his wife that] he slammed out of the front door and started walking up the road toward town.
>
> It was then that my mother had this vision. She had always...had a strong intuition of things about to happen.
>
> My father was well up the road when my mother ran screaming out onto the porch. "Early! Early!" She screamed his name. She clutched up her apron in one hand, and ran down across the yard and into the road. My father turned around. He saw her. For some reason, considering how angry he had been when he left, he waved at her. But he kept on going.
>
> ...[M]y mother had a vision of my father's end. All the rest of the afternoon, she was not herself, crying and nervous and upset. When my father was not back home by our bedtime, my mother hugged and clutched us, and we felt strange, not knowing what to do, because she had never acted like that.
>
> I remember waking up to the sound of my mother's screaming again. When I scrambled out, I saw the police in the living room; they were trying to calm her down. She had snatched on her clothes to go with them. And all of us children who were staring knew without anyone having to say it that something terrible had happened to our father.

It was morning when we children at home got the word that he was dead. My mother was hysterical. She was still hysterical at the funeral.

The insurance company refused to pay Mrs. Little the policy money on her husband's life. She began to buy on credit. This was a difficult thing to do, because her husband was strongly against the use of credit. "'Credit is the first step into debt and back into slavery,' he had always said. And then she went to work herself. She would go into Lansing and find different jobs—in house work, or sewing—for White people. They didn't realize, usually, that she was a Negro. A lot of White people around there didn't want Negroes in their houses."

Once when one of us—I cannot remember which—had to go for something to where she was working, and the people saw us and realized she was actually a Negro, she was fired on the spot, and she came home crying, this time not hiding it.

We would come from school sometimes and find [the state welfare workers] talking with our mother, asking a thousand questions. They acted and looked at her, and at us, and around in our house, in a way that had about it the feeling—at least for me—that we were not people. In their eyesight we were just things, that was all.

...My mother was, above everything else, a proud woman, and it took its toll on her that she was accepting charity. And her feelings were communicated to us.

She would get particularly incensed when they began insisting upon drawing us older children aside, one at a time, out on the porch or somewhere, and asking us questions, or telling us things—against our mother and against each other.

Then, about in late 1934, I would guess, something began to happen. Some kind of psychological deterioration hit our family circle and began to eat away our pride. Perhaps it was the constant tangible evidence that we were destitute.

About this time, my mother began to be visited by some Seventh Day Adventists...They would talk to her for hours at a time, and leave booklets and leaflets and magazines for her to read. She read them.

Before long, my mother spent much time with the Adventists...We began to go with my mother to the Adventist meetings.

Meanwhile, the state Welfare people kept after my mother. By now, she didn't make it any secret that she hated them, and didn't want them in her house. But they exerted their right to come...They would ask such things as who was smarter than the other. And they would ask me why I was "so different."

I can distinctly remember hearing "crazy" applied to her by them when...we all heard them call my mother "crazy" to her face for refusing good meat [from a Negro farmer]. It meant nothing to them even when she explained that we had never eaten pork, that it was against her religion as a Seventh Day Adventist.

...They told us, "She's crazy for refusing food." Right then was when our home, our unity, began to disintegrate.

It was about this time that the large, dark man from Lansing began visiting...The man, big and Black, looked something like my father. He was a single man, and my mother was a widow only thirty-six years old. She was having a hard time disciplining us, and a big man's presence alone would help. And if she had a man to provide, it would send the state people away forever.

...When the man came, our mother would be all dressed up in the best that she had—she still was a good-looking woman—and she would act differently, lighthearted and laughing, as we hadn't seen her act in years.

It went on for about a year. And then, about 1936, or 1937, the man from Lansing jilted my mother suddenly. He just stopped coming to see her.

[It] was a terrible shock to her. It was the beginning of the end of reality for my mother. When she began to sit around and walk around talking to herself—almost as though she was unaware that we were there—it became increasingly terrifying.

As my mother talked to herself more and more, she gradually became less responsive to us. And less responsible. The house became less tidy. We began to be more unkempt.

Soon the state people were making plans to take over all of my mother's children. She talked to herself nearly all of the time now, and there was a crowd of new white people entering the picture—always asking questions.

Eventually my mother suffered a complete breakdown, and the court orders were finally signed. They took her to the State Mental Hospital at Kalamazoo.

My mother remained in the same hospital at Kalamazoo for about twenty-six years. I would go to visit her every so often.

...Every time I visited her, when finally they led her—a case, a number—back inside from where we had been sitting together, I felt worse.

My last visit, when I knew I would never come to see her again—there—was in 1952. I was twenty-seven. She didn't recognize me at all.

She stared at me. She didn't know who I was.

Her mind, when I tried to talk, to reach her, was somewhere else. I asked,

"Mama, do you know what day it is?" She said, staring, "All the people have gone." I can't describe how I felt. The woman who had brought me into the world, and nursed me, and advised me, and chastised me, and loved me, didn't know me...

...We wanted and tried to stay together. Our home didn't have to be destroyed. But the welfare, the courts, and their doctor, gave us the one-two-three punch. And ours was not the only case of this kind.[11]

Individual Model

There is an individual model for assessing what is going on in the case above. This model is ego-centered. It is built on the concept of a person as a self-contained, "bounded, unique, more or less integrated motivational and cognitive universe, a dynamic center of awareness, emotion, judgment, and action organized into a distinctive whole and set contrastively both against other such wholes and against its social and natural background."[12] The ego-centered, self-contained person does not need anyone to complete her or his life. The self-contained person is an entity unto his or herself. The primary focus is the inner or subjective experiences of the individual, for example—the mind, feeling, thinking, and motivation. Pathology or problems, as well as health or wholeness, are located inside the individual. No one else can change a person; only the person can change him- or herself; and change comes through insight. Individuation, autonomy, self-mastery, and control are highly prized. In this model, the ego-centered individual can be adequately grasped and understood as a self-contained entity. The environment, community, and social structures serve as background or foil for the drama of the self. Meaning in life with significant others is created by the self-contained individual. In this model, the self-contained individual is all-important.

Systemic Model

There is another model for assessing what is going on in the case above. It is a systemic model and is relationship-centered. It is built on the concept that sociality or interrelatedness is the fundamental reality that underlies and gives rise to individual experience. We are born in and arise from relationships. This systemic model is based on the simple principle of linkage, the principle that everything in social life directly or indirectly links with everything else.[13] The self and the reality of persons is embodied and always embedded in social contexts and constituted by its many relations. Hence, the layered or many levels of connections and the quality of the bond between people are of vital importance when assessing what is going on. Contexts shape the meanings that individuals co-create. The primary focus is on intersubjective experiences (or the mind), power arrangements, and reciprocal influences that connect persons to themselves and others within a social web. We are ensembles of relations and integrators of meanings. Change comes through the shifts in the reciprocal connections between people, collaborative efforts, different social and cultural processes, and altered power position in a relationship system. Inner change is interwoven with the above-mentioned areas and with changes in the environment and culture—in which the individual plays her or his part. The environment, community, and meaning in life with significant others co-emerge through communication and purposeful activities. They are modified through reflection and the deliberation of interacting individuals. Sociality and the interrelatedness of persons—and personal contributions that support the system of relations, the web of life—are effective and all-important.

INSTRUCTIONS

---

a. Carefully and thoughtfully read through the descriptions for the individual model and for the systemic model, noting the differences between the two models.
b. Evaluate how this individual model helps to assess the context of Louise Little's life and difficulties. How does this model account for narrative agency and intercultural realities in this case?

In threesomes:

c. First, share your individual assessments of the models. Taking turns and without interruption, carefully listen to what your mates are saying about the case and the difference between the models.

d. Then, discuss and debate the difference the models would make in rendering culturally competent pastoral care. What happens to narrative agency and intercultural realities in each of the models?

e. Finally, in turn address the question: *From the perspective of each of the models*, what would be the different challenges for you to answer the question of Mark's gospel: "Who is my sister, mother, brother?"

This exercise is suited for the classroom or training program. It could be adapted for a daylong workshop.

Teaching Pastoral Care: Guidelines for the Use of Video Presentation or Slides

Video presentations help to create a context for teaching and learning. Through the use of selected video clips, observers can raise critical questions and match their expectations of what they see others do and do not do in contexts of pastoral care, narrative agency, systemic thinking, and intercultural realities. Students of pastoral care will be able to put their own learning into context by asking themselves what they do that others do not do, and why.

It is difficult, on average, to remain engaged with video (or slides) for longer than ten minutes. Try to show a clip (or clips) of not more than six to ten minutes in total length. The clip should show at least one intervention—that is, an attempt to change a difficult situation through purposeful talk, instruction, or an act or symbolic gesture.

Preparing to show a video clip from clinical practice

Before showing the video clip, answer the following questions succinctly—that is, stick to the questions and answer with only two to three minutes each (six minutes for question 1).

a. Describe the situation, and the people in it. Spell out the connections, as far as you know them, between significant actors within the context. What cultural, intercultural, and/or ethnic relations are involved? Describe the reciprocal behavior within relationships, and note where there may be an imbalance of power in these relationships due, for example, to greater physical strength, economics, cultural influence, or status. How do you see the relationship between the different sets of relationships? Describe the relationship between the pastoral situation and the wider social, cultural, and professional context. What is your theory, story, or hypothesis about what is going on in the situation (or social system)?

b. What is the problem the individual, family, or group was referred with? How is the problem framed or being defined, and by whom?

c. What, if any, connection do you see between the present problem and the relationships described above (see step 1)?

d. What is the issue you are addressing on the clip of tape you are showing? How was it chosen (e.g., was it an issue raised by an individual, family, or group or by you?), and why? What are you trying to achieve in this clip, and how?

e. Describe the social location of the pastoral caregiver. What is the relationship of the pastoral caregiver in terms of her/his actions and attributes (religious beliefs, gender, sexual orientation, ethnicity, age, class, etc.) to all you have described above?

Please note: When describing patterns of behavior, take care to be descriptive (i.e., Jane wore a full-length black dress and sat between both of her parents. Her head was bowed; her hands were clasped in her lap; and except for clearing her throat, she did not make a sound. Her parents talked about her, but never to her. This behavior was similar to last time). Avoid causal descriptions of behavior (i.e., so-and-so did this or that because…).

Preparing to show a video clip from a movie

a. Give the context and background of the film and the intent and purposes of the movie producer. Select the section of the video you want to show that best matches your teaching and learning objectives. The clip should not exceed more than ten minutes.

b. Identify your reasons for selecting this particular clip.

c. What particular scene or exchange within the clip do you want students to focus on and discuss?

d. Clearly identify the critical questions you wish the students to discuss and relate them to your teaching/learning objectives.

e. What is the plot? What norms and/or underlying values can be discerned? What forces operate to bind the actors together or keep them apart? How is narrative agency accounted for in the clip? Where is evidence of systemic thinking? How are intercultural realities acknowledged? These and other relevant questions and issues may be prepared for discussion in twosomes, threesomes or small groups.

f. Students may be invited to view the entire film when or as appropriate.

An example. Archie showed a video clip from Woody Allen's 1989 production of *Crimes and Misdemeanors*. It is a metaphysical comedy about how we conduct our lives in a time of moral confusion (i.e., there are no absolutes; we have to decide right and wrong for ourselves), a time that appears to be devoid of ultimate purpose. Archie picked a scene in which a respected doctor, an ophthalmologist and philanthropist named Judah, returns to the home of his youth. Judah has a flashback to a Seder. There is a debate around the table about whether or not God sees and punishes the immoral deeds done by humans. Several questions are raised in this video clip. Is there a moral structure to the universe? Is religion mumbo jumbo, or is there something to it? Does might make right, or does God see and punish evil deeds, such as murder? The questions are debated but not settled in this video clip.

This video clip was selected to stimulate discussion about the moral context of contemporary pastoral care. It allowed us to talk about narrative agency, that is, how we become selves through the decisions or choices we make. Hence, a moral structure for our lives emerges via our choices. We can appreciate that the significance of human freedom is in decision-making, but what norms guide our decisions? Is it the case that "honesty is always the best policy"? This is the advice Judah received from his rabbi.

We were able to link our observation of this video clip with questions such as, What is the moral context of our caring? Is it (the moral context) always discernable or clear? What responsibility (and skills) do we, as pastoral caregivers, have toward our own moral lives and the moral lives of others? How should we exercise (or exorcize) responsibility, and what are our limits? In whose name or by what authority do we act as moral and care agents in situations depicted in *Crimes and Misdemeanors*?

Students were invited to view the entire film. Most had already see it several times, but had not thought about or discussed its theological and pastoral implications in the context of a training program. The video clip lasted about seven minutes. The discussion lasted much longer.

Observing and analyzing a video clip

A visual experience, provided by use of a video clip or slide, can be very powerful if the participants are asked questions in such a way that they place themselves in relation to the video or slide material.

QUESTIONS

a. What event or series of events precipitated, or were thought to have precipitated, the presenting problems? What has changed? What is the bind? What is the wider context of the presenting problem?

b. What, if any, questions are being raised by the event(s)? What attachments and beliefs are affected? What emotions are or are not being expressed? What loyalties, if any, are being challenged? What solutions have already been tried?

c. How is the problem(s) being defined, by whom, and with what consequences?

d. What cultural or intercultural realities need to be taken into account? What power relationships need to be considered?

e. In a group, look for three ways in which verbal and nonverbal material confirm or disconfirm the hypothesis—that is, our hunch about what is going on.

f. What is the interaction between the hypothesis and the feedback from the individual, family, or congregation that would lead you to be stuck as the pastoral caregiver? Give three examples.

g. As a result of your questions and discussion, what contradictions appear to be emerging between the belief system and the behavior of the people involved in the situation?

h. What metaphors (images or symbols) does the individual, family, or congregation use to describe itself and its relationship to the Divine and to the presenting difficulty?

Selecting a slide, a narrative of classical painting for teaching purposes:

A narrative or classical painting is an underused yet excellent resource for teaching in pastoral care.[14] It can be very helpful in teaching students how to observe—take in a scene, give detailed description, notice contrast, and think in terms of frame (i.e., how something is framed). How does the frame around the painting work? How does it constrain what they see? The frame around a picture is analogous to the definitions that mark off, define, or distinguish a pastoral care situation from other situations of care. Learning to observe and enter a narrative or classical painting may be, in the teaching situation, analogous to entering a pastoral care situation from a particular standpoint. By narrative painting, I have in mind *The Execution of Lady Jane Grey* (1554) by French artist Paul Delarouche (1797–1856). Behind the painting is a narrative of the young Lady Jane Grey, Queen of England for only nine days at the tender age of sixteen. To explore the painting is to raise questions that lead to an exploration of her short life, her times, and the political-religious forces that sealed her fate.

A classical painting is one that is based on a historical event, such as the one just mentioned, or one based on an enduring mythical theme, as in *Bacchus and Ariadne* (1521–3), by the famous Venetian artist Titian (1487–1576), or *The Death of Actaeon* by Titian. These paintings are based on certain enduring life themes, many of which are relevant to pastoral care. Students can be encouraged to locate narrative and classical paintings and other works of art relevant to their own cultural background, or those of the people who turn to them for care. Students of pastoral care can learn to engage the aesthetic imagination as a resource for the provision of pastoral care.

A still frame or slide of a landscape, for example, may be used to invite the student to situate her or himself within it.

INSTRUCTIONS

a. Select the still frame or slide you wish to use. If it is a narrative or classical painting, become familiar with the story or layers of stories that lie behind it.
b. Invite students to sit quietly and observe the painting and jot down what they notice in the painting. They may be prompted by the simple question, "What do you see when you look?" It may take a few minutes for them to *enter* the painting.
c. After about ten minutes of looking, ask the students to stop writing. Remove the painting from view, and repeat the question, "What did you see when you looked?" Their responses can be written on the board. As the many responses begin to come in, something interesting begins to happen. Students discover a

range of perceptions, or ways of seeing that no one student was able to see. There is always more to see.

d. They may be invited to view the painting again. This time, they may notice some things that were missed the first time around.

e. The instructor may then invite them to think about questions such as the following:

- How is the painting framed?
- Where is there movement in the painting?
- What or where is the light source?
- What relationship or sets of relationships do you see?
- Which colors are used and with what effect? Are colors used to "achieve contrast"? to create shade? to unify? to balance? to focus?
- How is space used? Is there a rational organization of space?
- Where is the focus?
- What moods are created?
- What feelings and or themes are evoked?

These are some questions that will help observers enter into the painting the second time. By analogy, they will learn to ask certain questions in the pastoral situation—"How is the situation being defined? Is there movement or a shift in meaning in the situation? What or where is the light source, or from where does new meaning or illumination come? Where do we see hope? These are some possible uses of a narrative or classical painting or still frame.

General Learning Goals

Narrative Agency

The goal of narrative agency is to enhance the developing capacity for self-reflexivity and be able to identify themes that help determine narrative agency—in the way problems are defined and relationships are thought about.

1. **Problem definition:** Things that are defined as real become real in their consequences, according to W. I. Thomas.[15] The learning goal is to gain an understanding and appreciation of the way problems are defined by help seekers and to notice the relationship between the definition of situations and resources. Also important is gaining appreciation for the reciprocal relationship patterns within pastoral situations and how different sets of relationships impinge on one another, including aspects of culture, race, sexual orientation, gender, class, and power.

2. **Conceptualize relationships:** The goal here is to be able to conceptualize a relationship between persons and between the pattern within the family, group, or congregation and a problem presented by the family or congregation.

Systemic Thinking

The goal of systemic thinking is to identify connections between the binds people are in and their beliefs, emotions, and behavior; and to find ways to do things differently.

1. **Appreciate the power of observation:** The goal here is to increase our appreciation of the power of observation, description, noticing, and the role of questions in evolving new ways of seeing in pastoral care.

2. **Conceptualize interventions:** The goal here is to be able to conceptualize and increasingly be able to use possible interventions in work with individuals, families, groups, congregations, or social systems.

Intercultural Realities

The goal here is to identify intercultural realities that mark differences between persons from different cultural backgrounds, and to appreciate the influences of intracultural realities between persons within the same ethnic or cultural group.

1. **Identify cultural resources** that have not been identified in order to raise critical questions about pejorative ideas such as "different," "does not fit or belong," "strange," "bad," "mad," "outsider," or "foreigner," and to learn to appreciate how such descriptors are a part of interactive processes that may be important indicators of change and point to different or new resources.

2. **Increase awareness of reciprocal processes:** The goal here is to develop an awareness of the effect of culture on the individual, family, congregation, or situation, and on oneself as a professional pastoral care provider; and to recognize the impact of oneself (social location) on the individual, family, congregation, or situation and be able to use this knowledge constructively.

Conclusion

We are pastoral care theologians who live and work in very different cultural contexts. Yet the one world we share is estranged— broken and scarred by corporate greed, hunger, terrorism, international conflict, and other barriers that are alien to community.

Fear of difference breeds violence, and violence breeds fear and mistrust and counterviolence. These forces work against the recognition of our common humanity and fundamental relatedness. We choose to explore what it means to work together and across the forces that divide our world. We base our thinking on an intercultural sibling metaphor derived from the gospel of Mark's eschatological family of God. Who are my mother and my brothers? Whoever does the will of God is my brother and sister and mother (Mk. 3:33,35). We are related to one another, not by blood ties, clan, tribe, or national origin, but in doing the will or pleasure of God. Our contemporary question was this: *How is it possible for women, men, and children from different cultural and spiritual backgrounds to come together and struggle against common forms of oppression, and in that process become siblings by choice?* This question leads to a complex reading of our contemporary situation. We have suggested that siblings around the world and in every language cry for food, water, and nurturing relationships of justice, love, power, and freedom. There are seemingly insurmountable obstacles to becoming siblings by choice. We have shown that we live amid deceit and fear, complex and conflicting forces that can alienate or destroy us. Yet we believe that our lives are fundamentally interrelated and grounded in spiritual resources that are greater than those forces. We have used the lenses of narrative agency, systemic thinking, and intercultural realities to uncover those resources and explore the challenge of becoming siblings by choice. In this last chapter, we have provided opportunities to explore further the possibilities of becoming siblings by choice. We have a treasure in earthen vessels to repair breaches in human relationships and resolve conflict. The source of that treasure is the Divine Spirit. We are gifted with spiritual resources that give rise to a shared moral vision that can renew and inspire us to do better than we have. The exercises provide opportunities to cross borders, acknowledge differences, and engage the contradictions that are a part of our common life. The exercises enable a search for deeper meanings that can enrich and bring renewal. We choose to become siblings across differences and together struggle to do God's pleasure.

Notes

Chapter 1: Siblings in Struggle—Siblings by Choice?

[1] See Mitch Albom, *Tuesdays with Morrie: An Old Man, a Young Man, and Life's Greatest Lessons* (New York: Doubleday, 1997), 157.

[2] *The Oxford Encyclodecdic English Dictionary* (Oxford: Clarendon Press, 1991), 1346.

[3] Private communication from Professor Norman Gottwald, 4 October 2003.

[4] Norman K. Gottwald, *The Tribes of Yahweh: A Sociology of the Religion of Liberated Israel, 1250–1050 BCE* (Sheffield, England: Sheffield Academic Press, 1999), 237.

[5] Ibid., 240.

[6] Gottlob Shrenk, "Will," in *Theological Dictionary of the New Testament*, Vol. 3, ed. Gerhard Kittel; trans. and ed. Geoffrey W. Bromiley (Grand Rapids, Mich.: Wm. B. Eerdmans, 1965), 54–62.

[7] Mary Ann Tolbert, "Introduction to the Gospel According to Mark," *The New Interpreters Study Bible: New Revised Standard Version with the Apocrypha* (Nashville: Abingdon Press, 2003), 1801.

[8] Ibid., 1812.

[9] Mary Ann Tolbert, *Sowing the Gospel: Mark's World in Literary-historical Perspective* (Minneapolis: Fortress Press, 1996), 240.

[10] Ibid., 47.

[11] Ibid., 262.

[12] Ibid., 14.

[13] Howard Thurman, *The Search for Common Ground* (Richmond, Ind.: Friends United Press, 1986), xiv.

[14] Howard Thurman, *The Creative Encounter: An Interpretation of Religion and the Social Witness* (Richmond, Ind.: Friends United Press, 1954), 152–53.

[15] Thurman, *Search for Common Ground,* 42.

[16] Ibid., 103.

[17] Community Childhood Hunger Identification Project, 1995, http://www.frac.org/html/hunger_in_the_us/hunger_studies2.html.

Chapter 2: Autobiographical Perspectives

[1] Fray Angelico Chavez, *The Lady from Toledo* (Fresno, Calif.: Academy Library Guild, 1960), 7.

[2] Last words of Friedrich Von Hugel (born Italy 1852, died England 1925), cited in Sylvia Shaw Judson, *The Quiet Eye: A Way of Looking at Pictures* (London: Aurum Press, 1982).

[3] Abraham J. Heschel, *The Prophets* (New York: Harper & Row, 1962).

Chapter 3: Transcending Barriers Alien to Community

[1] From Howard Thurman, *The Search for Common Ground: An Inquiry into the Basis of Man's Experience of Community* (New York: Harper and Row, 1971), 103: .

[2] *San Francisco Chronicle*, 21 October 2001.

[3] Inga-Britt Krause, *Culture and System in Family Therapy,* Systemic Thinking and Practice Series (London: Karnac Publications, 2002), 2.

[4] Reinhold Niebuhr, *Moral Man and Immoral Society* (New York: Charles Scribner's Sons, 1932), xx.

[5] Steven Winn, "Lies Are No Longer Damned Lies: Americans Reduced to Expecting Deceit," *San Francisco Chronicle*, 8 June 2003.

[6] Joan Chittister, "From Where I Stand," *National Catholic Reporter: The Independent News Weekly*, vol. 1, no. 9, 27 May 2003.

[7] Reinhold Niebuhr, *Moral Man and Immoral Society* (New York: Charles Scribner's Sons, 1932), xii.

[8] Inga Britt Krause, *Therapy Across Culture* (London: Sage Publications, 1998), 115.

Chapter 4: Moral Vision in a Climate of Diminishing Trust

[1] *Kandahar: Journey into the Heart of Afghanistan,* directed by Mohsen Makhmalbaf, New Yorker Video, 2003.

[2]Martin Bright, "Heartbroken of Kandahar," *Guardian Unlimited*, 4 November 2001, www.guardian.co.uk.

[3]*Kandahar—Journey into the Heart of Afghanistan*, http://www.kandaharthemovie.com.

[4]Bright, "Heartbroken of Kandahar."

[5]George M. Furniss, *The Social Context of Pastoral Care: Defining the Life Situation* (Louisville: Westminster John Knox Press, 1994), 16.

[6]Diane Schoemperlen, *Our Lady of the Lost and Found: A Novel* (New York: Penguin Books, 2001), 255.

[7]Dan Bar-On, *Furcht und Hoffnung. Drei Generationen des Holocaust* (Hamburg: Europäische Verlagsanstalt 1997); Gabriele Rosenthal, ed., *Der Holocaust im Leben von drei Generationen; Familien von Überlebenden der Shoah und von Nazi-Tätern* (Giessen: Psychosozial Verlag 2004, 3. ed.); Wolfgang Schmidbauer, *Ich wusste nie, was mit Vater ist. Das Trauma des Krieges* (Reinbeck bei Hamburg: Rowohlt Verlag 1998).

[8]Helm Stierlin, *Delegation und Familie – Beitrag zum Heidelberger familiendynamischen Konzept* (Frankfurt am Main: Suhrkamp, 1978).

[9]Ivan Boszormenyi-Nagy and Geraldine M. Spark, *Invisible Loyalties: Reciprocity in Intergenerational Family Therapy* (New York: Brunner/Mazel, 1973), 67.

[10]Ibid., 67–68.

[11]A. Massing, G. Reich, E. Sperling, *Die Mehrgenerationen Familientherapie*, trans. Ursula Pfaefflin, 4th ed. (Göttingen: Vandenhoek and Ruprecht, 1999), 21.

[12]Ruthard Stachowske, *Mehrgenerationentherapie und Genogramme in der Drogenhilfe. Drogenabhängigkeit und Familiengeschichte* (Heidelberg: Asanger Verlag, 2002).

Chapter 5: Invisible Forces Determining Human Existence

[1]John Henrik Clarke, Introduction to *The Middle Passage*, by Tom Feelings (New York: Dial Books, 1995).

[2]Rodney J. Hunter, ed., *Dictionary of Pastoral Care and Counseling* (Nashville: Abingdon Press, 1990), 848.

[3]Henry Louis Gates, Jr., and Cornel West, *The Future of the Race* (New York: Vintage Books, 1996).

[4]Donna Haraway, "Situated Knowledges: The Science Question in Feminism and the Privilege of Partial Perspective," *Feminist Studies* 14, no. 3 (fall 1989): 579.

[5]Pierre Boudieu, *Outline of a Theory of Practice* (Cambridge, N.Y.: Cambridge University Press, 1977), 72.

[6]Ibid.

[7]Suman Fernando, *Race and Culture in Psychiatry* (London and Sydney: Croom Helm, 1988), 17.

[8]Paula Allen-Meares and Sondra Burman, "The Endangerment of African American Men: An Appeal for Social Work Action," *Journal of the National Association of Social Workers* 40, no. 2 (March 1955): 268.

[9]Ibid., 5.

[10]Tom Feelings, *The Middle Passage* (New York: Dial Books, 1995), 1.

[11]Ibid.

[12]Lerone Bennett, Jr., *Before the Mayflower: A History of the Negro in America 1619–1964*, rev. ed. (Baltimore: Penguin Books, 1966), 40.

[13]Ibid.

[14]Russell Jacoby, *Social Amnesia: A Critique of Contemporary Psychology From Adler to Laing* (Boston: Beacon Press, 1975).

[15]Ibid., xv–xvi.

[16]The term *pentimento* was shared with me in an informal conversation with a student, Ann Sonz Matranga. See also, Lillian Hellman, *Pentimento: A Book of Protraits* (Boston: Little, Brown, 1973).

[17]Peter Fryer, *Black People in the British Empire: An Introduction* (London: Pluto Press, 1988), vii.

[18]John Lukas, *Historical Consciousness or the Remembered Past* (New York: Harper & Row, 1968), 10.

[19]Walter Wink, *The Powers That Be: Theology for a New Millennium* (New York: Doubleday, 1998), 1.

[20]David Hume, *Essays Moral, Political and Literary,* ed. T. H. Green and T. H. Gross (Darmstadt: Scientia Verlag Aalen, 1964), 252n. See also, Suman Fernando, *Race and Culture in Psychiatry* (Worcester, England: Billing and Sons, 1988), 10.

[21]Ronald Takaki, *A Different Mirror: A History of Multicultural America* (Boston: Little, Brown, 1993), 52.

[22]Noel Ignatiev, *How the Irish Became White* (New York: Routledge, 1995), 41.

[23]Craig Calhoun, "Habitus, Field, and Capital: The Question of Historical Specificity," in *Bourdieu: Critical Perspectives,* ed. Craig Calhoun, Edward LiPuma, and Moishe Postone (Chicago: University of Chicago Press, 1993), 70.

[24]Mary Donovan Turner and Mary Lin Hudson, *Saved from Silence: Finding Women's Voice in Preaching* (St. Louis: Chalice Press, 1999).

[25]Taylor Branch, *Pillar of Fire: America in the King Years 1963–65* (New York: Touchstone, 1998), 137–38.

[26]William Julius Wilson, "Cycles of Deprivation and the Underclass Debate" (paper presented at the ninth annual Social Service Review at the School of Social Service Administration, University of Chicago, May 21, 1985), 3.

[27]See Lawrence Bob, James R. Kluegel, and Ryan A. Smith, "Laisse Faire Racism: The Crystallization of a Kinder, Gentler, AntiBlack Ideology," in *Racial Attitudes in the 1990s,* ed. Steven A. Tuch and Jack K. Martin (Westport, Conn.: Praeger, 1997), 16–42; Lawrence Bob and James R. Kluegel. "Status, Ideology, and Dimensions of Whites' Racial Beliefs and Attitudes: Progress and Stagnation," in *Racial Attitudes in the 1990s,* ed. Tuch and Martin, 93–120. [However, as noted by Jennifer Hochschild, in the same surveys, "Blacks also rank whites higher than the other three ethnicities on all six ratings. African Americans rank their own race most prone to accept welfare, more patriotic and work oriented than Hispanics, and more intelligent and peaceful than both Asians and Hispanics." See Hochschild, *Facing Up to the American Dream: Race, Class, and the Soul of the Nation* (Princeton, N.J.: Princeton University Press, 1995), 111; see also, William Julius Wilson, *The Bridge Over the Racial Divide: Rising Inequality and Coalition Politics* (New York: Russell Sage Foundations, 1999), 131.

[28]Wilson, *Bridge Over the Racial Divide,* 19.

[29]William H. Grier and Price M. Cobbs, *Black Rage* (New York: Basic Books, 1968).

[30]Cheryl A. Kirk-Duggan, *Exorcizing Evil: A Womanist Perspective on the Spirituals* (Maryknoll, N.Y.: Orbis Books, 1997), 152.

[31]Bill Adler, *The Wisdom of Martin Luther King* (New York: Lancer Books, 1968), 95.

[32]This information was conveyed to me in a private communication with the new defending attorney on 3 May 1999. See also, Larry D. Hatfield, "Vietnam Vet Babbitt Executed," *San Francisco Examiner,* 4 May 1999.

[33]Hatfield, "Vietnam Vet Babbitt Executed."

[34]Michelle Locke, "Babbitt Scheduled to Die at Midnight," *San Francisco Examiner,* 3 May 1999.

[35]Allen-Meares and Burman, "Endangerment of African American Men," 269.

[36]See Suman Fernando, *Race and Culture in Psychiatry* (London: Croom Helm, 1988), 140–41; World Health Organization, *Report of the International Pilot Study of Schizophrenia,* vol.1 (Geneva, Switzerland: World Health Organization, 1973); World Health Organization, *Schizophrenia: An International Follow-up Study.* (London: Wiley, 1979); Jafar Kareem and Roland Littlewood, eds., *Intercultural Therapy: Themes, Interpretations and Practices* (Oxford: Blackwell Scientific Publications, 1992).

[37]David Weber, "Killer's Cousin Opposes His Upcoming Execution," *Boston Herald,* 17 March 1999.

[38]Hatfield, "Vietnam Vet Babbit Executed."

[39]Allen-Meares and Bunnan, "Endangerment of African American Men," 269.

[40]Jay Severin, "A Life for a Life," MSNBC Home Page Web Site, May 7 1999.

[41]Marian Wright Edelman, "An Advocacy Agenda for Black Families and Children," in *Black Families,* ed. Harriette Pipes McAdoo (London: Sage, 1981), 291.

[42]Ibid., 292.

[43]John L. McAdoo, "Involvement of Fathers in the Socialization of Black Children," in *Black Families,* 225.

[44]Ibid., 226. See also, S. Price-Bonham and P. Skeen, "A Comparison of Black and White Fathers with Implications for Parents Education," *The Family Coordinator* 28, no. 1 (1979): 53–59.

⁴⁵Archie Smith, Jr., *The Relational Self: Ethics and Therapy from a Black Church Prespective,* (Nashville: Abingdon Press, 1982), 195–99.

⁴⁶Ibid.

⁴⁷Barbara Moore, "The Death of Two Daughters: Grieving and Remembering," accessed on Web site http://www.und.nodak.edu/dept/philrel/jonestown/daughters.html.

⁴⁸Jeannie Mills, *Six Years with God* (New York: A & W, 1979), 26.

⁴⁹Fumitaka Matsuoka, *The Color of Faith: Building Community in a Multicutural Society* (Cleveland, Ohio: United Church Press, 1998), 3, 12, 18, 23.

⁵⁰Ibid., 18.

⁵¹Ibid., 12.

⁵²Ibid., 11.

⁵³Ibid., 23.

⁵⁴Marian Wright Edelman, *Lanterns: A Memoir of Mentors* (Boston: Beacon Press, 1999), 117.

⁵⁵2 Corinthians 4:7.

⁵⁶This is from a 1998 Christmas letter from American Church historian, Eldon G. Ernst.

⁵⁷Ibid.

⁵⁸Ibid.

Chapter 6: Gender Change and Cultural Traditions

¹George Furniss, *The Social Context of Pastoral Care: Defining the Life Situation* (Louisville: Westminster John Knox Press, 1994), 1.

²Judith Lewis Herman, *Trauma and Recovery* (New York: Basic Books, 1992), 3.

³Ibid.

⁴Will and Ariel Durant, *The Lessons of History* (New York: Simon and Schuster, 1968), 11.

⁵Humberto R. Maturana and Francisco J. Varela, *Autopoiesis and Cognition: The Realization of Living* (Boston: Reidel, 1980).

⁶Anthony Horowitz, *Myths and Mythology* (New York: Simon and Schuster, 1985), 127–39; William F. Russell, *Classic Myths to Read Aloud* (New York: Crown Publishers, 1989), 112–17.

⁷It is interesting how many artists have dwelled on the theme of Ariadne as deserted lover in the European history of arts; see Jane D. Reid, *The Oxford Guide to Classical Mythology in the Arts, 1300–1990s* (New York and Oxford: Oxford University Press, 1993).

⁸Questioning persons are those who have not settled or decided their sexual identity. They are still questioning whether they identify with being male or female or identify themselves in some other way.

⁹Hermann Kern, *Labyrinthe. Erscheinungsformen und Deutungen. Fünftausend Jahre Gegenwart eines Urbilds* (München: Prestel Verlag, 1982).

¹⁰Heide Goettner-Abendroth, *Die Goettin und ihr Heros* (Muenchen: Frauenoffensive, 1980), 16.

¹¹Barbara Walker, *The Women's Encyclopedia of Myths and Secrets*, (San Francisco: Harper SanFrancisco, 1983), 55.

¹²Jeremy Taylor, *The Living Labyrinth* (New York/Mahwah, N.J.: Paulist Press, 1998), 197.

¹³Goettner-Abendroth, *Die Goettin und ihr Heros.*

¹⁴Hermann Kern in his major work on labyrinths reads the story historically. Ariadne gave to Theseus the knowledge of the labyrinth dance (the thread) which means the Minoan culture of Crete, which was more elaborated and higher than the culture of Greek winners (heroes), was subdued to the successors. The dance in Delos. The labyrinth dance, symbolizes the experience of danger and the solution of dangerous situations, a dance of initiation for young people who have to learn 'the way of life'. In the story of Theseus, there are many indications for initiation. After he goes into the labyrinth, and returns he can become the King of Athens.

¹⁵See also Inga-Britt Krause, *Therapy Across Culture* (London: Thousand Oaks; New Dehli: Sage, 1998). Krause reports on matrifocal, matrilineal societies and the importance for therapists to enlarge their own understanding of kinship in diverse cultures, including the knowledge of ethnography.

¹⁶Furniss, *Social Context,* 2.

Chapter 7: Death and the Maiden

[1]Peter Pitzele, *Our Fathers' Wells: A Personal Encounter with the Myths of Genesis* (San Francisco: Harper SanFrancisco, 1995), xxiv.

[2]Ariel Dorfmann, *Death and the Maiden* (New York: Penguin Books, 1991).

[3]From ibid., 59. Also supplemented from the 1994 movie, *Death and the Maiden*, starring Sigourney Weaver, Stuart Wilson, and Ben Kingsley (New Line Home Entertainment, 2003).

[4]North American Theologian James Poling has addressed the strong tendency of male perpetrators very well in his book *The Abuse of Power: A Theological Problem* (Nashville: Abingdon Press, 1991), in which he portrays two of his cases in his own work with victims and perpetrators of domestic violence. He also discusses the theological impact of the abuse of power in regard to the image of God and concepts of christology.

[5]By "intercultural," we mean a setting in which a member of one ethnic group facilitates a process or therapeutic intervention that empowers a member of another ethnic group to make beneficial decisions. See Jafar Kareem and Roland Littlewood, eds., *Intercultural Therapy: Themes, Interpretations and Practice* (Oxford: Blackwell Scientific Publications, 1992), 11.

[6]David W. Augsburger has defined a difference between sympathy, empathy, and interpathy in *Pastoral Counseling Across Cultures* (Philadelphia: Westminster Press, 1986). "In interpathy, the process of knowing and 'feeling with' requires that one temporarily believe what the other believes, see as the other sees, values what the other values" (p. 31).

[7]Inger Agger, et al., *Trauma and Healing under State Terrorism* (London and New Jersey: Zed Books, 1996).

[8]Stuart Turner states: "Only if the therapist or group has developed some coherent understanding of the social and political context in which they are working, can they really start to address the ideological needs of their clients." See Turner, "Therapeutic Approaches Survivors of Torture," in *Intercultural Therapy*, ed. Kareem and Littlewood, 167.

Chapter 8: Complexity and Simplicity in Pastoral Care

[1]The Very Reverend H. C. N. Williams, Provost of Coventry, *The Pictorial Guide to Coventry Cathedral: Cathedral Church of St. Michael* (Stockport, England: North Western Printers, 1963), 6.

[2]Primo Levi, *Survival in Auschwitz: The Nazi Assault on Humanity* (New York: Simon and Schuster, 1996), 90.

[3]Ibid., 89.

[4]Alan Travis, "Stephen Lawrence's legacy: Confronting racist Britain," *The Guardian*, 25 February 1999.

[5]"Full text of Jack Straw's statement to Parliament," *The Guardian*, 24 February 1999, special report, The Stephen Lawrence Case.

[6]Jay Rayner, "The hidden truth behind race crimes in Britain," *The Observer*, 18 February 2001.

[7]Ibid.

[8]Rodney G. King was a young black man, age twenty-five, who was beaten by police officers at a traffic stop in South Central Los Angeles on March 3, 1991. He was hit more than fifty times by officers wielding their batons. The bones holding his eye in its right socket were broken, and he suffered eleven broken bones at the base of his skull. The police officers reported that King appeared to be on PCP. However, subsequent tests showed that King had neither PCP nor alcohol nor any other drug in his system. The attack on Rodney King was deemed as racially motivated by Los Angeles Mayor Tom Bradley, and by civil rights leaders because of the "bigoted remarks" of the officers and because the beating fit the pattern of abusive behavior by police toward blacks. The Los Angeles police officers and supervisors downplayed the level of violence used against King, claiming that he suffered only cuts and bruises of a minor nature. "A Perspective on the Rodney King Incident," *Los Angeles Times*, 19 March 1991, A20.

[9]C. G. Montefiore and H. Loewe, eds., *Rabbinic Anthology* (New York: Schocken Books, 1974), 462.

[10]Gerhard Kittel, ed., *Theological Dictionary of the New Testament*, trans. Geoffrey W. Bromiley, vol. 1 (Grand Rapids, Mich./London: Eerdmans, 1964), 511.

¹¹Ibid.

¹²Ceslas Spicz, O.P., *Theological Lexicon of the New Testament*, trans. James De Ernest, vol. 1 (Peabody, Mass.: Hendrickson, 1994), 242.

¹³Ibid.

¹⁴Ibid.

¹⁵Ibid.

¹⁶Ibid.

¹⁷Ibid.

¹⁸Kittel, *Theological Dictionary of the New Testament*, 511.

¹⁹See Paul Tillich, *Love, Power and Justice* (New York: Oxford University Press, 1960).

²⁰Ibid., 25.

²¹Ibid., 15.

²²James Wm. McClendon, Jr., *Biography as Theology* (Philadelphia: Trinity Press International, 1974), 78.

²³Mitch Albom, *Tuesdays with Morrie: An Old Man, a Young Man, and Life's Greatest Lesson* (New York: Doubleday, 1997), 166.

²⁴Desmond Mpilo Tutu, *No Future Without Forgiveness* (New York: Doubleday, 1999), 148.

²⁵Sharon Lamb, "Individual and Civic Notions of Forgiveness." Information obtained from http://tigger.uic.edu/~lnucci/MoralEd/articles/lamb.html on May 15, 2004.

²⁶See Inger Agger, *The Blue Room: Trauma and Testimony among Refugee Women: A Psycho-Social Exploration* (London: Zed Books, 1992).

²⁷Albom, *Tuesdays with Morrie*, 164.

Chapter 9: Resources for Becoming Siblings by Choice

¹Clifford Geertz, *Local Knowledge: Further Essays in Interpretive Anthropology* (New York: Basic Books, 1983), 59.

²This vignette comes from Larry Kent Graham, *Narratives of Care Among Lesbians and Gays* (Louisville, Ky.: Westminster John Knox Press, 1997), 103–4.

³This vignette comes from D. Mark Wilson, "I Don't Mean to Offend, but I Won't Pretend: Experiences of Family Life for Gay Men within an African American Church," in *Tending the Flock: Congregations and Family Ministry*, by K. Brynolf Lyon and Archie Smith, Jr. (Louisville, Ky.: Westminster John Knox Press, 1998), 167.

⁴Ibid., 160.

⁵Ibid., 150.

⁶Graham, *Narratives of Care*, 59.

⁷Fray Angelico Chavez, *The Lady from Toledo* (Fresno, Calif.: Academy Library Guild, 1960), 7.

⁸Mitch Albom, *Tuesdays with Morrie: An Old Man, a Young Man, and Life's Greatest Lesson* (New York: Doubleday, 1997), 164.

⁹Linda Joy Myers, Ph.D., *Becoming Whole: Writing Your Healing Story* (San Diego, Calif.: Silver Threads, 2003), 161.

¹⁰Alex Haley, *The Autobiography of Malcolm X* (London: Penguin Books, 1965).

¹¹Ibid., chap. 1.

¹²From Clifford Geertz, *Local Knowledge: Further Essays in Interpretive Anthropology* (New York: Basic Books, 1983), 59.

¹³Brian Swimme and Thomas Berry go further and suggest the "Cosmogenetic Principle." This principle "states that vast webs of pathways exist potentially at every place in the universe." It links everything with everything else. This principle is the story of the unfolding universe. "Every living being of Earth is cousin to every other living being. Even beyond the realm of the living we have a common origin in the primordial Flaring Forth of the energies from which the universe in all its aspects is derived." Brian Swimme and Thomas Berry, *The Universe Story: From the Primordial Flaring Forth to the Ecozoic Era. A Celebration of the Unfolding of the Cosmos* (San Francisco: HarperSanFrancisco, 1992).

¹⁴Archie Smith, Jr., "Classical Paintings in the Teaching of Pastoral Care," in *Art as Religious Studies*, ed. Doug Adams and Diane Apostolos-Cappadona (New York: Crossroad, 1987), 180–89.

¹⁵W. I. Thomas and D. S. Thomas, The Child in America: Behavior Problems and Programs (New York: Alfred A. Knopf, 1928), 572.

Index of Names

Index of Topics

Printed in the United States
22705LVS00007B/97-120